ANXIETY WARRIOR

A Scared Man's Path to Success and Happiness

BRIAN BENEDUCE

Anxiety Warrior
A Scared Man's Path to Success and Happiness

iUniverse books may be ordered through booksellers or by contacting:

iUniverse
. 1663 Liberty Drive
Bloomington, IN 47403
www.iuniverse.com
1-800-Authors (1-800-288-4677)

ISBN: 978-1-5320-7787-6 (sc)
ISBN: 978-1-5320-7788-3 (e)

Library of Congress Control Number: 2019908740

Print information available on the last page.

iUniverse rev. date: 07/12/2019

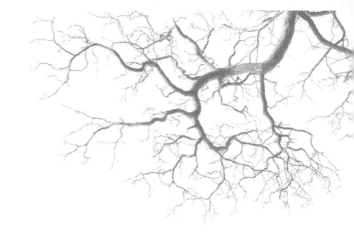

Dedication

This book is dedicated to Robbie, my best friend and wife,
and to Jennifer and Michael, my wonderful children.

Courage is not the absence of fear,
but the learning to act in spite of it.

~ Theodore Roosevelt

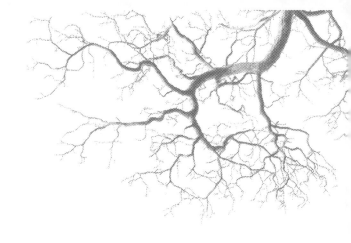

Foreword

I'm best known for writing hero stories. Whether these heroes are scaling monstrous waves like the Coast Guard crew in *The Finest Hours*, or whether they are running head first into the smoke and fire to save lives moments after bomb blasts in *Patriots Day*, they all share a common trait – strength of character.

I've found that many of us are capable of performing extraordinary acts when we are called upon in times of great stress. But such bravery is fleeting. They are merely moments that don't allow us the fortune of time to thoroughly weigh the consequences of our actions. The idea of rising each day to face my worst possible fear over and over again is a foreign concept to me, but it's exactly what Brian Beneduce confronts every morning.

As a severe agoraphobic, Brian is in constant struggle with his subconscious mind and in that mind lives a beast that is hell bent on destroying his life. The inner battles that are waged in this book are terrifying to read and painful to comprehend.

Yet, Brian's story is not a tragedy. It is a triumph. It's a testament to one man's unwavering will to succeed and tame those dark, paralyzing thoughts induced by anxiety and panic.

How did this perpetually frightened individual become a multi-millionaire and proud family man? That answer can be found here in these pages and in his own honestly gripping words. Add the name Brian Beneduce to the list of heroes that have survived and thrived against insurmountable odds.

— **Casey Sherman**, New York Times Bestselling Author of *The Finest Hours*

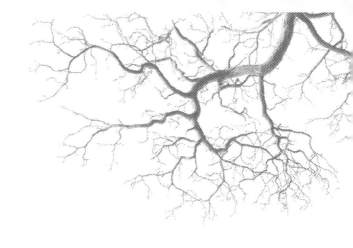

Prologue

THE
HONEYMOON

I had just married the most beautiful woman on earth and I
wanted to die. My childhood sweetheart and blushing bride
Robbie knew I had a fear of flying, but she had no idea what was
going through my mind when we boarded the plane. I imagined
what she was thinking about; spending time together, our first as
husband and wife on the tropical island of Antigua. I should have
been thinking about that too. After all, the hard part was over. I
had managed to keep my panic disorder under control while in
church. My throat didn't close when we exchanged our vows. I

didn't collapse in front of all our friends and family members. And I didn't puke on my rented dress shoes. I kept it together.

We took our seats and strapped in for our flight to paradise. Robbie patted my shoulder and I did my best to smile back. As circulated air got pumped into the plane, I immediately began to sweat. The idea of being trapped for 6 hours and belted inside an aluminum tube at 35,000 feet was a fate worse than death. That's not melodrama.

As the plane rumbled down the runway and lifted off into the morning sky, terrifying thoughts starting seeping into my brain. "I have to get off this plane," I told myself. I was crawling out of my skin and losing control. The Thing, this three headed beast inside me, was now taking over. Suddenly, I felt the urge to charge the cockpit and demand the pilot land the plane. Then I looked at the plane door. Was that a better bet? Could I just throw the flight attendant aside and push myself out into the blue sky and away from the confines of this plane?

Will I run up and down the aisle screaming at the passengers like a mad raving lunatic? Maybe I will kill one of them with my bare hands?

I squeezed the armrest of my seat until my knuckles turned white as I wrestled with the beast, a beast that wanted to kill me and everyone on board. On a level of 1 to 10, my anxiety level was at 9 and pushing toward 10. As my wife sat peacefully beside me with her head in a magazine, her husband was fighting the battle of his life. In my mind, the Thing had me in its talons, thrashing me as its claws dug into my skin. I wanted to give in to the beast and that meant doing something irrational and possibly murderous. But I fought back, swinging my hammer back at the monster to regain some control. The three headed beast recoiled and then retreated to the far reaches of my mind.

I had managed to bring my panic level down to a 7. This meant that I would not make any attempt to put Robbie or the other passengers in danger. Instead, I began praying to God. I prayed for a lightning strike or some other calamity to take the plane out of the sky and end my torment. At that moment, I wished for death. I looked around the cabin at our fellow passengers and decided that I absolutely hated every one of them -- they were calm, relaxed, and many slept soundly. I glanced over at Robbie and realized she had fallen asleep also.

Most people who have a fear of flying - fear crashing, but not me. A crash was exactly what I prayed for. When I tell others about this reaction, they think I'm joking -- but I swear I am serious. I don't want to die; I just need relief from the perpetual torture. Think about the terror 200 passengers might suddenly feel if they thought their plane was about to crash. It's what I feel while we're cruising along calmly. I just might look around the plane and shout at them, *"There, you see? That's what I've been feeling since we took off!"*

This is what it's like to be Scared to Death.

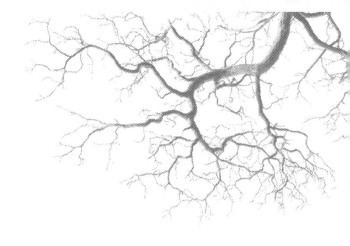

DOCTORS

It is easy to be brave from a safe distance.

~Aesop

The clinical definition for an anxiety and panic attack reads like this:

> *"...an acute psychobiologic reaction manifested by intense anxiety and panic. Symptoms include heart palpitations, shortness of breath, dizziness, faintness, profuse diaphoresis, pallor of the face and extremities, gastrointestinal discomfort, an intense feeling of eminent doom or death.*

Attacks usually occur suddenly, last from a few seconds to an hour or longer, and vary in frequency from several times a day to once a month. Prolonged panic and anxiety can cause agoraphobia which is a condition where the person is afraid to leave his/her so-called safe place..."

But for most of my adult life, I just called it "The Thing." As far back as I can remember, from my childhood into my twenties, I would experience massive panic attacks that I could not describe to anyone else – not my family, no one. Maybe it was because I didn't want to look weak. I have always valued strength and found it embarrassing and shameful to lose control. And since I really didn't know what was wrong with me anyway, I learned that blaming my health -- especially my heart -- could be the perfect scapegoat.

I remember sitting in hospitals and in doctors' offices many times while the doctors focused intently around the performance of my heart and my irregular heart palpitations. Many times the emergency room doctors would keep me there for hours hooked up to all sorts of wires and EKG machines, carefully monitoring my blood pressure and my heart rate, making certain all was fine before they let me leave. But I admit, I was not being totally honest with them. I couldn't tell them that my heart problems always revolved around my profound *FEAR*. I needed to convince them there was more of a physical reason. You see, if I acknowledged the fear, it would have revealed a chink in my armor. My pride would not allow me to accept that.

Through the years, I have had many hospital visits and most of the time they were short, because as soon as I arrived, I'd immediately feel the relief of help being near, and I would begin to calm down. I have never had a doctor tell me I was experiencing anxiety or panic attacks. Never. Not once. But admittedly, I never gave them all the right information they needed to make a proper diagnosis. It was too embarrassing for me. When asked, my answers to their questions were usually vague.

"No Doc, nothing really happened."

"I really don't know what's wrong with me."

"No, I didn't have 12 cups of coffee."

"Yes, I promise to get my heart checked by my family doctor as soon as I get home."

When I was younger, I was once prescribed beta blockers to help with the palpitations. Beta blockers are drugs often given to cardiac patients to treat heart palpitations, angina, high blood pressure and other related conditions. I took them for a while but deep down I knew that they weren't treating the problem -- or should I say treating the root of the problem. So I just stopped taking them.

And I once had a nurse ask me if I was seeing a psychologist, accusing me of bringing this all on myself. Was this all self-inflicted? Was I crazy? I was into my late twenties at the time and was spending lots of time alone as my wife was frequently on the road working as a flight attendant for Eastern Airlines. I remember leaving the office and spending a long evening lost in my own thoughts, not arriving back at home from the hospital until five o'clock that morning feeling deeply depressed. Because how could I, the proud, strong man I was, be doing all this to myself on purpose? Could the nurse be right? Was I just imagining this THING?

When I finally found the courage to get professional help, my psychiatrist came to the conclusion that I was a victim of my own ego feeding upon itself. I don't know if he realized that I was suffering from anxiety and panic or not, as he never actually used those words. But he did give me a homework assignment. He asked me to read Tom Wolfe's novel, *A Man in Full*. I remember that as I read the book, I wondered why, out of all the books in the world, he gave me this one to read. The story is essentially about a man with a massive ego trying to be everything to everyone. His ego was divided between good (confident) and bad (self destructive). I figured I must have an awful lot of this last one.

But did this explain why I couldn't be alone? Why I feared all things? Was my problem my ego?

The psychology was over my head at the time. I couldn't analyze my condition while under constant attack by the Thing.

The beast was always lurking. One night, while staying at a friend's apartment in New York City, I awoke early in the morning gripped by sudden fear. The Thing had come out of its cave to kill me in my sleep. I felt a strong urge to walk out on the balcony, lift my body over the railing and jump. But again, I fought back. I fought for my life. I pulled the belt off my bathrobe and tied it tightly around my wrists and then to the armchair of the couch, anchoring me. I could feel an invisible force pulling at the belt as I tethered myself to the large piece of furniture. My wrists burned as the beast pulled at the ties with its teeth.

"I am stronger than you," I muttered. "I'm gonna live today, dammit!"

I had never entertained a single suicidal thought in my life, but I wasn't sure if The Thing wouldn't make me jump anyway, or more accurately, push me. But what had triggered this raging impulse to propel myself off the balcony to my death? My manic behavior had grown out of fear. This time it was the fear of burning alive.

"We're on the 20th floor," the Thing whispered to me. "If the building erupts in flames, you'll have no way out. You'll be burned alive."

My greatest fear at that moment was waiting for what I believed was the inevitable to happen and having no control over the outcome. This was exactly what had induced my panic attack on the plane bound for my honeymoon. The beast was trying to convince me that I could decide my fate, that I had control over the way I lived and the way I would die.

But I had no control at all. I gripped the side of the couch with my tied hands and hung on. For more than an hour, I shook the couch and swore at myself as if under the spell of demonic possession. The bathrobe I wore was soaked in sweat and my arms felt the depleted strength and soreness of a tug of war. Finally, as the sun rose over the New York City skyline, I had somehow managed to bring my panic level down.

When this Thing takes control of my mind, I experience over a hundred different uncontrollable, painful urges shooting through my head at the same time. All of these feelings, while clearly psychological, caused many physical problems. And once the physical problems kicked in -- heart palpitations, sweaty palms, hands shaking like a leaf -- then my brain would take over with deep feelings of panic.

I was sick all the time, suffering from a cold or the flu as the intense stress would cause my immune system to crash. It was a terribly vicious cycle, and it still is. And without the right tools to know how to combat it, to battle the beast, it's a horrible way for anyone to go through life.

It is not an out-of-control ego. It is not self-inflicted. It is agoraphobia.

To sufferers of agoraphobia, horrible thoughts come to you no matter where you are -- fear of passing out when driving a car, or on the train in front of people, or in church walking up to communion, or in public places like restaurants, supermarkets, malls -- basically everywhere. It's fear of leaving your safe place.

I used to test myself and see how far I could walk through a store without running for the exit. But constantly fighting with yourself is not the way to deal with anxiety and panic. The first step toward fixing this affliction is to just let it happen, feel the fear, accept it, and learn exactly what it is all about. Only after you understand the true nature of the beast can you ultimately defeat it.

Without any formal medical support, I created my own system of determining the severity of these panic attacks on a 1 to 10 scale. I have never experienced a 10. To me, that number equals death.

One out of ten people suffer from this disorder in the United States. If you are one of them, please understand that although it may feel like it, you are not alone.

Now let me show you how I was able to overcome it.

2

THE INNOCENT

When one has the feeling of dislike for evil, when one feels
tranquil, one finds pleasure in listening to good teachings; when
one has these feelings and appreciates them, one is free of fear.
~ **Buddha**

The Thing targeted me early. Studies suggest that less than 1% of children are predisposed to agoraphobia. Erratic, withdrawn behavior in children is sometimes labeled as a form of autism, but that was not true in my case and countless others like me.

I was born in Cranford, New Jersey in 1961 and our family lived in Dunellen, in the central part of the state. Dunellen was a typical small city -- barely a square mile wide with plenty of parks and easy access to the highway and close to New York City.

My dad was a blue-collar, hard-working guy who fit right in with the makeup of the neighborhood. In fact, I remember him always working two jobs as long as we lived there. My mother also worked a part-time job, but she was far more interested in raising her kids. Both my parents grew up in Brooklyn in the 1950's, and embraced the traditional, classic American values of that era and were eager to use them to raise their own family.

When I turned five, I was sent to kindergarten at St. Mary's, the local Catholic school. During that time, even as a young boy, I could feel the racial tension of the day as low income whites and blacks fought over low paying jobs and a stake in the city. The strained relations would boil over a few years later when places like nearby Plainfield erupted in deadly riots that would burn parts of Jersey over three nights and four days.

I remember feeling the stress and anxiety it brought although I didn't understand it. Even at this age, I remember being in tune with my anxiety and fear. The Thing hovered around me constantly waiting to strike.

One day while I was in the second grade, we had been assigned a class project that involved cutting a picture from one page and pasting it in the right place on another. I had somehow completely misunderstood the assignment and instead, colored in the area that was supposed to be glued. Most people can relate to this situation, especially when recalling their childhood, but the small beast growing inside me took what was an innocent and yet embarrassing moment to the extreme.

After the assignment, the nun called each student by name and had us come up to the front of the class to have our work examined and checked off. Although I had many friends in the class, I absolutely hated the idea of standing up in front of all my schoolmates. I could not bear that kind of attention, even during a daily exercise like this.

When I realized the mistake I'd made with my assignment, I panicked. I didn't have any glue, so I scribbled with my yellow crayon as hard and frantically as I could until the waxy build-up was thick and sticky, and then I pressed the picture into the right place, hoping it would stick long enough to have the project approved and let me return to my desk unnoticed. I prayed that this last-minute fix would get me through. Even at seven years- old, I can vividly remember all the classic symptoms and stages of anxiety and panic attacks coming on -- sweating, heart palpitations, shaking -- but back then, to me, this was normal. I thought that every kid my age was living with The Thing.

As luck would have it, I was the last student in my row to be called to the front of the class. All I needed was for Sister Mary to look at the paper for five seconds and I'd get my check mark. I could feel my throat closing as I presented my work to the nun. But the waxy yellow crayon just wouldn't hold like glue, and my hastily-attached little picture slipped off and fell helplessly to her desk. The nun scowled, pointed her crooked finger, and ordered me to stand in shame at the front of the class.

I was so terrified that I lost control of myself and defecated in my pants. I wanted to run or at least waddle out of class and find my way to the nurse's office as quickly as possible. But instead, I stood there feeling terrified and ashamed as the nun checked off the remainder of my classmates' work. She then turned her attention back to me, slashed a ruler across the back of my hand and ordered me to take my desk.

I returned to my seat as instructed, my eyes welled with tears. I stared down at the desk, hoping that no one would smell the terrible odor emanating from my chair. There was nowhere for me to escape. The Thing had me trapped. As the nun was preparing for the next lesson, she spun her head, crumpled up the bridge of her nose and asked,

"Did somebody soil their pants?"

And of course, every finger in the room pointed at me.

As I reflect back, I know two things for sure: first, there's no doubt this incident deepened my social anxiety and secondly, though I liked school, it was the first step toward a future of really hating schoolwork.

The nuns at St. Mary's practiced negative reinforcement, when the only way a child like me could thrive was through re-assurance and love.

I have always been a pleaser. I longed to please both my father and mother from an early age, and I enjoyed the feeling of making them proud. Whether it was fixing a mailbox, shoveling snow, or just cleaning up after a birthday party, I thrived on their approval. There was nothing more important to me.

But with my classmates, the only I way I could get their approval, or so I thought, was to make them laugh. So as odd as it was for a kid to hate being the center of attention, I would often talk out of turn. At St. Mary's, we had to go to church every day, and if you got caught talking, a nun would make a fist and plant it in your back so hard the whole church would vibrate. I was on the receiving end of that punishment more than once.

In the summer of 1969, my father came home one afternoon and announced that he had been offered a new job at a medical plastics company called Becton Dickinson in Canaan, Connecticut. Because of the rising racial tensions and crime in our city at the time, I learned he had been looking to relocate our family for quite a long while.

And what a wonderful culture shock it would be for an eight-year-old boy!

Suddenly, we were living in a wonderful ranch house with three acres of land. For a little city boy like me, moving to Canaan was absolute heaven -- the school was big, yards were big, and there was a true sense of freedom. There were even 10,000 acres of land behind my new house called Canaan Mountain, and I would come to explore every square inch of it.

Canaan was a refuge for me. No longer was I the boy who had crapped his pants in second grade, or the kid who the nuns beat regularly for pleasure. I was able to make many new friends, play outside until after dark every night, and with the help of all the older kids in our new neighborhood, I learned how to make go-carts out of wagons, ride mini-bikes, play baseball, play pond hockey and overall, just have a hell of a great time running around in the woods.

I also learned a lot about myself -- I learned I loved to be alone.

One of my favorite pastimes was to build a fort out in the woods and just sit inside for hours. Here I was safe, secure and relaxed. Inside my fort everything was great, and all was always well in this world. With a hammer, wood and some nails, I had built an impenetrable fortress to protect myself from the Thing. My fort was my kingdom and it kept the beast at bay.

But I couldn't stay in my fort forever, this the beast knew. When I went home or went out in public, the Thing was always ready to pounce.

On Sunday nights, my parents would often go out on errands and to the movies together, and leave me alone with my older sister Laura and younger brother Steven. Initially, I felt relaxed while watching the classic 70's TV line-up of *The Lawrence Welk Show, Wild Kingdom,* and *The Wonderful World of Disney.*

Then my parents would stroll out the front door and suddenly, my throat would begin to close. My sense of reality had shifted with my parents gone, even if it was only for a couple of hours. Our normal nightly routine had changed and my anxiety grew. They represented my home base, where I would be safely out of reach from the beast.

I would silently pray for them to stay, and I remember being very upset when they'd leave. My parents had no way to know the severity of the attacks I was dealing with, and how every time they left, the anxiety deepened. Though I wanted them to stay, I didn't want them to know why. And I'm not sure I could have explained it anyway.

Anxiety and panic feeds on itself in a vicious cycle, and when you are a child, you don't possess any of the tools you need to cope with these situations. It was on these Sunday nights that I first started to believe there was something terribly wrong with me -- all the time. Why did I do this to my parents? I was a pleaser -- I couldn't bear to upset them. I did not understand. The guilt and embarrassment was starting to build.

Canaan was a very safe town. There were no strangers lurking about, and everybody knew everybody else. Yet still, I was constantly in fear.

But that didn't stop me from trying to enjoy the fruits of my childhood. I joined the Boy Scouts, which I loved despite the fact that camp was 45 minutes away from home, away from my safe place. I enjoyed all the activities during the day, but at night, I was terrified as the Thing rose from my subconscious to tell me that something awful was about to happen to me.

The anxiety I felt was overwhelming, yet I did not dare show it. I remember creating excuses about things I had to go and do whenever I heard there would be a sleepover coming up.

Tommy was one of my best friends, and he and his family lived on a huge 20-acre lot that had a camper on site. I loved hanging around with Tommy, but I hated sleeping over in his camper, and couldn't bear to say anything to him or anyone about it. Again, I wasn't afraid of the walls closing in, or werewolves, or maniacs coming out of the forest to attack us, I was simply afraid of my own thoughts. This was the period of my life when the *"what ifs"* began:

"What if my throat closes?"

"What if I can't breathe?"

"What if I pass out?"

"What if...?"

Embarrassment had taken control of my life.

Looking back on it now, although I have so many great childhood memories, I regret not having more. Now decades later, it's still easier to remember the fear.

EMERGENCY!

Dispatcher: *Squad 51, informant reports toxic chemicals in the tanker, use caution.*

    Dr. Kelly Brackett: *Squad 51, this is Rampart. Can you send us some EKG?*

    John Gage: *Ten-four, we're transmitting EKG. We're sending you a strip. Vitals to follow. Pulse is 160, the victim is in extreme pain, Rampart. V-fib!*

Paramedic Roy DeSoto: *Patient is in V-fib! Rampart, we have lost the victim's pulse, beginning CPR....*

    — From the opening credits to the TV show *Emergency!*

If you are old enough, you might remember the 1970's television show *Emergency.* The show was about paramedics who would put their lives on the line every week while running around Los Angeles saving dying people.

I hated that show.

It was a great TV program for a kid. It had action, suspense, police cars, and fire engines. What wasn't to like? But for me, I couldn't watch any TV show about the medical profession. The minute the paramedics showed up at the scene, and the victim was either passed out, hyperventilating, dizzy, unconscious, feeling chest pain, hallucinating, or experiencing any one of a hundred other symptoms, my anxiety level would shoot through the roof.

"Hey, that's me, that's what I have," I told myself. "I'm going to pass out, get rushed to the hospital and die just like them."

To be honest, my dislike extended to all hospital TV shows, or any other drama that over the course of telling its story found its way into a hospital or doctor's office. I couldn't watch any of those programs without believing the victim on each show was me.

Thank God I didn't have the Internet or WebMD when I was growing up!

Panic and anxiety attacks are a mental problem first and physical problem second. However, I can tell you firsthand that the pain and physical symptoms at times would become so intense that I truly believed I was dying from some serious disease. When you don't know what you have or what's wrong, your brain has the tendency to search until it finds what it thinks is the most logical answer. It's looking for its "aha" moment.

Every time your eyes begin to burn or your stomach starts to ache, you start to hope there is something physically wrong with you and that you now have the symptoms that will prove it. When you don't know what you have, your anxiety becomes magnified because you believe your body is out of control. You find yourself in a constant search for answers, and anything you can latch onto helps ease your stress. You pray you'll discover the "aha" moment again, because that last "aha" moment, though it provided temporary relief, didn't work out so well.

Ironically, every time I got sick, it came with an unexpected feeling of relief. *Yes! Thank goodness I'm sick! There really is something wrong with me! I feel like this because I have XYZ Disease!* The Thing could become a creature with a medical name, something that I could possibly explain, understand, and control.

But sadly, after every illness, something terrible would happen -- I would get better.

I admit this is hard to understand, but children and adults who suffer silently from this affliction know exactly what I'm talking about. They pray to find the real reasons behind their irrational thoughts and look for answers around every corner, even television shows.

When I was ten years old, I bought a booklet in a penny candy store in downtown Canaan that featured a picture of a man standing with his arms up holding a barbell over his head. This guy looked incredibly powerful and his muscles were gigantic! The booklet offered detailed information on getting strong and promised that if the instructions were followed, I would look just like him. With a physique like his, I could certainly defeat the Thing, or so I thought. As a child, I had already recognized that there was something wrong with me. And I remember thinking to myself that all my problems -- the nervousness, the fear, the panic, the anxiety -- were all because I was a scrawny, weak kid. I convinced myself that if I followed the advice in this booklet and got stronger, I would be bigger and tougher and all my fears and problems would just melt away and the beast would retreat to its cave forever.

I took the booklet home and read it cover to cover, and then I read it again. I immediately began doing push-ups and sit-ups just like the booklet said I should. We didn't own a set of weights, but I was still able to do many of the strength-training exercises in their place. I would work on the muscles in my chest, my arms, my back and my shoulders every single day. When my parents' friends came to visit, I'd work through my routine alone in my room, then prance around the house with my shirt off waiting for someone to comment how big I looked. They always did, but I assume they said it just to please me. I looked pretty much the same as I always had, but I felt great. I felt like a super hero.

The first time that I truly overcame my fear was when I ran over underground nest filled with yellowjackets in the woods. The insects had burrowed themselves in a rodent hole that I had mistakenly stepped on. My younger brother was a few feet behind me and he felt the fury of the bees once they'd been aroused. As I continued to run, I heard screams behind me. I turned around and saw the yellowjackets descending like small fighter planes around my brother. I'm petrified by bees and my instincts told me to keep running and get my father's help. But suddenly, I felt my legs running in the opposite direction, back toward my brother, back toward danger. I grabbed him and pulled him away from the frenzied insects that were stinging him all over his body. I brushed the bees off with no concern for my own safety and rushed him out of the woods. I could feel the bees inside my shirt and shorts, but for some unknown reason, they kept their stingers away from me and I escaped unscathed.

I had surprised myself with my own bravery, something I didn't believe I'd possessed. Gaining strength and being physically tough became my version of the chainmail suit, a set of invisible armor that would protect me from all beasts, both real and imagined.

It would not be the last time I would have to defend my brother. We had many neighborhood friends we played baseball with almost every day in the summertime. Skirmishes within our groups of friends were normal -- boys will be boys as they say. Whenever my brother would get into a squabble with any one of my friends, I would always come to his aid ready to fight. But I would pray to myself it wouldn't come to real fisticuffs. I might have acted and looked tough, but inside, I was terrified.

One of my best friends at that time was named Nate, and he was the toughest kid in our group. His parents had divorced and I remember he carried around a ton of anger. The second toughest kid in town was Jimmy, and he was twice the size of

Nate. I remember Jimmy starting something with me one time, and I remember Nate jumping to my defense and smashing Jimmy square in the face. I'll never forget how scared I was or the humiliated look on Jimmy's face as he ran home. A few days later, my brother mouthed off to Nate during a pick-up basketball game. It was just a war of words until my brother decided it would be a great idea to spit at him. Nate totally lost it -- and charged him. My brother hopped on his bike and rode away, leaving me behind, per the code of the neighborhood, to defend his honor. I chased Nate down as I was expected to, but I did not hit him. I just begged and pleaded with him to please just leave my little brother alone. Nate did eventually cool off and back down but I will never forget that sensation of crippling fear that knotted itself in the pit of my stomach. If Nate had turned around to me and said, *"OK, let's go,"* I don't know what I would have done. I am grateful he didn't.

My school in Canaan was five times bigger than my school in New Jersey, and there were a lot of big kids around. I wanted so badly to not only fit-in "size wise", but to be normal and not my usual nervous self. I felt that I was finally emerging from my shell, when my home base, my safe place began to crumble.

My father, who was always trying to do better for himself and our family, received an offer to manage a manufacturing company that molded plastic bottles and parts in Providence, Rhode Island, and he accepted it. I was leaving Canaan. I felt sick to my stomach. I bawled my eyes out. Our Connecticut town was paradise for a kid: mountains, little girl crushes, baseball, fishing and neighborhood friends. I was leaving all that behind for an uncertain future.

When we moved to Rhode Island, the first friend I made at my new school was named Bill. He was a neighborhood kid who thought I was pretty cool. It didn't take me long to figure out Bill didn't have many friends and was terrible at sports. I think he was drawn to me because I was the new kid and because I was small and obviously wasn't one of the cool kids. All the popular kids were big, looked tough and played sports. One of those students was a tough, scary-looking kid named Reggie who wore an army jacket all the time and smelled awful, like he lived in a foxhole. He was big, and also a star member of the school's wrestling team.

One day in gym class, the teacher announced our activity that day would be wrestling. And of course with my luck, I was randomly matched up against Reggie who not only outweighed me by at least 25 pounds, but he also smelled like cigarettes. I was terrified. As expected, he pinned me to the mat in less than two seconds. I really had no idea how to fight him off, and as I was going down, I blindly thrust my palms up into his face and struck him square in the nose. It was an accident, but that didn't stop a sudden burst of blood from shooting across the mat. Reggie was humiliated, furious, and fully prepared to destroy me. The gym teacher dove in quickly and broke us up. Thank God. If there had been a real fight, I probably would have been killed.

Here I was, a sophomore in high school, nose to nose with Reggie, face bloodied, looking me square in the eye.

"Okay. Let's go, after class," he snarled.

With only two or three friends in the whole school to protect me against Reggie's tough group of friends, I was doomed. My mother would pick me up after school on occasion, and Reggie would see me as he walked past and would flip me off. My mother was alarmed, and asked what was going on, and of course I would shrug it off and say he was just some odd, new friend. Reggie had the reputation for starting many fights, and finishing them very quickly. My goal was to avoid Reggie everywhere, all the time, at all costs.

I was a scared, panic-stricken kid with zero confidence again. My body armor was gone. The Thing had mobilized Reggie to play my daily tormentor, and he did it with relish.

I was now living in day-to-day survival mode. To get out of fighting Reggie, I had to blend in with the rest of the kids and disappear -- like a chameleon. I learned that when I hung around with the nerds, I could look and act like a nerd. When I hung around with the potheads, I could look and act like a pothead. When I hung around with the jocks, I could look and act like a jock. To my surprise, this chameleon act helped me become more popular with everybody -- including a lot of girls. It's funny how fear and anxiety drove me to adapt and become a relationship-driven person. It would be a skill I would carry into business and sales and use for decades to come. And by the way, I never did need to fight Reggie; in fact, we became friends.

I made another new friend then, too. He loved to work out, and was a motorhead with a great car, so a bunch of us would pile in and go to a nearby gym to train. Although I had given away my weights long ago, that desire to increase my physical strength had never left me. I never did throw away that little booklet I bought at the candy store, and in fact, still have it tucked away safely to this day. By the time I reached my junior year in high school, I had gained 20 to 25 pounds of muscle. I was also getting stronger and could bench press 315 pounds. I finally felt like I was becoming one of the guys. My confidence was slowly building along with my popularity. But the beast was biding its time, watching and waiting.

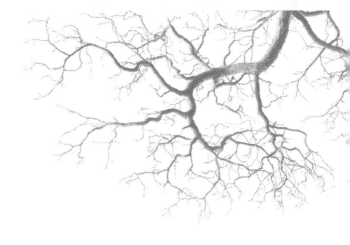

ALL THAT JAZZ

Don't fear mistakes. There are none.

~ **Miles Davis**

In high school, the gym became my new fortress. It was a place where I felt safe, secure and most importantly, in control.

The stronger I got, the less anxiety I felt. I was regaining my confidence and sometimes that led me straight into trouble.

I had grown from scrawny kid to starting varisty football player thanks to the long hours that I had dedicated to myself in the gym. I was a teenager filled with testosterone and I was constantly seeking out new and violent ways to test my manhood. I had been a slave to the Thing for so long, I was now eager to show others what I was capable of.

I got hurt during a football practice, dislocated my elbow and shoulder, and was forced to stand on the sidelines one Saturday to watch our team play. When halftime ended, I walked with the team back to the field from the locker room when someone from the opposition's grandstands cat-called down at me.

"Hey punk! You suck!"

Even though I had one arm in a sling, I glared back at him with all the self-assurance in the world.

"Fuck you!" I shouted back.

The kid flew down out of the grandstands toward me and I heard those magic words once again.

"Oh yeah? You want to go?"

I was strong. I was cool. I was pumped and by this time I had been in and even won a few fights. And oh hell yes, I did. I did want to go.

The two of us walked into the end zone and fists flew. The adrenaline was pumping through my veins with such force that my badly-injured arm didn't hurt one bit. We fought until police officers closed in and restored order.

I did some soul searching after the fight. Instead of feeling tough, I felt weak because it showed that I had a lack of control. So I decided to channel my anger and energy in the gym where I could release some of my aggression without hurting anyone.

The Thing stayed away from me while I was in the gym, my fortress, but that didn't mean the beast was far behind.

I sought out other activities that would pull me out of my comfort zone, force me to perform my daily activities without a net. I had an ear for music and joined the high school jazz band. I played trumpet and our group won a competition to perform in London. At this point, I didn't know that I had a fear of flying because I'd never flown anywhere before. Somehow I was able to detach myself from thoughts of doom. The six hour flight across the Atlantic Ocean was nothing like the panic stricken journey with my wife years later. The only problem I faced in England was the fact that a buddy and I lost our passports while talking to and trying to impress some girls. We ended up getting kicked out of the band. That would be my last trip to Europe.

I dated many different girls in high school, wooing them with my muscular physique, keen sense of humor and my own car, a Nova SS with the rear end raised and long pipes that came out the back. I exuded confidence but it was just a disguise to mask my fear and self doubt. The disguise seemed to work especially with the girl who would become the love of my life.

"I was fifteen years old when I first met Brian," says Robbie Beneduce, Brian's wife of more than 30 years. "What drew me to him originally was the fact that he was a cute, popular athlete who wore his letterman jacket around school."

Robbie thought I was too cocky at first, and she almost ran the other way. She was unlike anyone I'd ever met. She was a bit of a hippie. Robbie was beautiful but different. She was slim, athletic, and introverted.

"I was extremely intimidated by him, but he was endearing and sweet," she remembers. "The first time Brian came over to my house to meet my parents, he walked in and seemed so self-assured. My mom and dad loved him right away."

Robbie and I became inseparable in high school, but I knew that she would one day go off to college and because of my poor grades; I'd be relegated to working in my father's factory as a mechanic. I didn't like school and my grades reflected that. In one of my less than stellar progress reports, my teachers wrote that I had poor preparation, poor attendance, poor test scores, a lack of serious approach to my studies, and a lack of participation.

The mask I'd worn in the hallways was removed and exposed once I sat down at my desk. I felt that I was still that scared little child who had crapped his pants in front of all his classmates and this was my way of rebelling against academia and fighting off the Thing.

My stress level increased when Robbie went to college and I wasn't a part of that. Although the University of Rhode Island was a short car ride away, it was a world away from my life and my future. We split up when she began living on campus as we declared that we both wanted to see other people. This was a great idea in theory, but I didn't realize the heartache it would cause.

"The trouble started when I joined a sorority during my sophomore year," she recalls. "Brian had his friends keeping a close eye on me while I was enjoying the college experience. When I'd attend a frat party, suddenly Brian would show up."

I was trying to give Robbie her space but I was also fearful of letting go. Most couples experience these feelings in similar circumstances but mine were exacerbated by severe anxiety and agoraphobia. Robbie had become my safe place also and now there was a good chance that I would lose her.

THE SKI TRIP
FROM HELL

The brave man is not he who does not feel

afraid, but he who conquers that fear

~ **Ernest Hemingway**

Anxiety has a wretched, heartbreaking habit of straining your relationships and ruining your favorite activities by turning them into something frightening. I watched helplessly as all the things I learned to love and enjoy throughout my childhood slowly began to manifest themselves differently as I grew older. Finding reality became part of every activity I chose to undertake. Was I going to enjoy doing it as I always had, or would the anxiety drive me to hate this, too?

As a teenager, my panic and phobias had reached an all-time high leaving me in a state of constant ready-alert.

One day my friend Joe called and asked, "Hey Brian, what do you say we get the guys together and go up to New Hampshire for the weekend, rent a place and do some skiing?"

"Oh, yeah! I am in!" I answered.

I loved to ski. But I couldn't possibly let Joe know that the thought also absolutely terrified me. The Thing began whispering in my ear. *You have to drive all the way to New Hampshire, stay in some cabin in the middle of nowhere with no help available for miles? How are you gonna possibly survive this?*

It was like Boy Scout camp all over again.

We picked the worst possible time to leave -- five o'clock on a Friday afternoon -- and fought traffic all the way through Massachusetts into New Hampshire. All the great 80's rock bands like Boston and Kansas played on the radio as we travelled, and we sang along like we were on stage somewhere. The music, and the case of beer we bought for the ride, helped keep my friends cool and mellow; and that helped me cope with the building stress. And yes, I was driving. I couldn't possibly let anyone else be in control.

The Kancamagus Highway snakes its way for almost 60 miles around, over, and through New Hampshire's White Mountain National Forest. It's a tricky drive during the day in the summertime, never mind at night in the dead of winter. The farther along the highway I drove, the higher my anxiety level rose.

I tried to smile even though my heart was racing at 100 miles per hour. Again, I could hear the beast in my head.

What happens if you pass out and we crash into those trees, or go over these guardrails and plunge into an icy ravine?

I kept my hands on the wheel and my eyes on the road as I felt myself lurching the car ever slightly to the edge. I fought my dangerous impulses and kept a steady hand in a desperate attempt to tame the Thing.

We stopped for food at around ten o'clock. I felt like I had been driving for days, and hadn't seen a set of oncoming headlights in over an hour. I prayed that we had to be close. I didn't think I could drive much more.

"How much longer? I asked my friend Joe. "We almost there?"

"Yeah, almost," he replied. "Only about another hour and a half."

I could hear the beast laughing in my head.

Somehow, I continued to bear down and we eventually made it to the cabin. There was a second car that was following us that night that became hopelessly lost along the trip (of course there were no GPS units or cell phones back then), and arrived hours later after stopping several times to ask for directions. What Joe didn't know was that I didn't need directions. A good, card-carrying agoraphobic always does his research and memorizes exactly where he is going before he leaves his house. As we pulled into the parking lot, I looked ahead and couldn't believe my luck -- our rental was right next door to a hospital. Instantly, I felt a rush of relief and my anxiety level dropped like a stone. I laughed knowing that I had defeated the Thing, if only temporarily.

I was suddenly in a good mood, and after we tossed our bags into our rooms, we all came together in the kitchen for another round of beer, shots and air guitar. We partied and acted like complete fools until about 1:30 a.m. when everyone finally burned out and started to crash.

I disappeared into my room alone. Some might think that with panic and anxiety problems, having friends around at night would help. But for me, it was just the opposite. These guys were my best friends whom I had hung out with almost every Friday night. If I was forced to get up in the middle of the night and act like a complete panic stricken maniac, I had to make sure none of them would be around to witness my embarrassing transformation.

I only slept about three and a half hours when as expected, a level 9 panic attack spiked out of nowhere. The beast wasn't beaten yet.

I learned later on that alcohol masks anxiety. But as you sober up it bounces back like a rubber band to excruciating levels. It was the middle of winter and I was bathed in sweat. I couldn't stop thinking about being alone out there in the middle of the wilderness. I looked out the window and couldn't see a single light. I monitored and counted every breath -- in and out, in and out -- and sincerely feared I would do something harmful to myself or others. The only thought that helped was the knowledge that the hospital was just a half mile down the road. But the Thing wouldn't let go.

What if you run out the door toward that hospital and don't make it? How would they know that you were lost out there somewhere in the middle of the woods?

The morning sun finally lifted over the mountains and I quietly slipped out the back door before anyone else was awake. I hopped in the car and drove the half mile down to the hospital, which was actually a small medical clinic. I didn't want to go in, but I just needed to have a look around. I needed to make sure it was really there, that it wasn't some kind of mirage.

The building appeared to be open, but I talked myself out of checking the hours that were posted on the front window. I thought it better to assume and pretend they were open even if they weren't as I wasn't sure I could handle any bad news. Plus, there was a 24-hour food mart next door so I had another place to go if I was in trouble just in case. That was good enough.

After breakfast we headed over to Wildcat Mountain for our first day of skiing. I loved to ski, but what I hate is everything else that has to do with skiing. I hate the crowds. I hate the lines. I hate the lifts. I hate the gondolas. I hate the possibility of the gondolas getting stuck. What if! What if!

I also despised the thought of getting lost in the woods. It's not a normal type of "lost" sensation that most people might feel, but a sensation of complete and utter panic. What would I do if I reached a level 9 panic attack? Would the Thing compel me to ski off the side of the mountain?

When we first arrived I was physically shaking from the adrenaline that was coursing through my body, and my friends gave me a hard time, assuming I was having a bad reaction to the cold.

"Oh, come on Brian. Look at you! It's not that cold!"

I was trembling so bad that when I sat on the chairlift, globs of snow shook loose off the bottom of my skis. I remember looking back behind us every time the chairlift would slow down usually to let a small kid get on. I was so angry with them all. And God forbid if one of those little kids would fall getting on the chairlift -- what would happen then? What would I do? I had to get off this thing. I was breathing so rapidly that the condensation coming out of my mouth made me look like a smoke stack compared to everyone else.

"Is everything OK, man?" Joe asked.

"Yea, of course," I answered. "I feel like shit, though. I think I just partied a little too much last night, that's all."

I was lying, smiling, humming to myself and experiencing a panic attack 60 feet in the air. And the lies and pretending always made it much worse.

By the time I got off the chairlift, I was exhausted and hadn't even completed my first run. And just as I felt my anxiety start to ease back from a 9 down to a 7, I realized we were only halfway up the mountain; this was just the midpoint. And of course, all my friends wanted to go all the way to the very top. Sure they did. After all, there was a bar up there.

"So, what do you say, Bri?"

"Yes, that sounds great!," I replied with faux enthusiasm. "Let's get to the top of the mountain!"

The second part of the ride up the chairlift was just as excruciating as the first part, and became instantly worse when one of my buddies decided it would be a good idea to swing the chair back and forth. I laughed and pretended it was fun, but deep down, all I could think about was where I would jump off. Every fifteen feet or so I would rationalize that if I jumped here, I could survive and probably only break my legs. I debated if that would be preferable to enduring the panic of swaying in the chair. But I knew that if we stopped and the lift got stuck, there was no way I could sit there for an hour and wait for help to arrive. There was no question I would choose to jump under those circumstances.

"You are in control of how you live and how you die," the beast whispered. "Why wait for the inevitable?"

It was now only 10:30 in the morning when we arrived at the bar at the top of the mountain and I needed a drink. After all the Jack Daniels, rum and beer we consumed the night before, our stomachs ached and none of us really wanted to drink anything else, but when you're a teenager and indestructible, you don't let old-fashioned common sense get in the way. But I drank to help my anxiety subside, not to have fun. So for every one beer my buddies had, I downed three.

Our first trip down that day was on one of the most challenging hills on the mountain, a double black diamond trail from top to bottom. It starts with a 12-foot drop and zoom -- you're on your way!

But while I was skiing, I was free. I am a good skier and have no fear or apprehension when gliding down almost any hill at any speed. It's funny, because whether riding dirt bikes or skiing challenging trails, all the fear and anxiety happens either before the fact or after the fact. The "what ifs," "yeah buts," and "oh nos" are products of the subconscious mind – the Thing. The adrenaline goes right to the roots of your anxiety tree and makes you believe you had no business ever leaving your house, never mind skiing.

The analogy as it relates to adrenaline is the same in the gym. When I was growing up, if you could bench press 315 pounds, then you were the man. There were only two kids in my school who could do it, and they were huge. I weighed a measly 165 pounds. I knew I could bench 300, but whenever I sucked it up and went for 315, the adrenaline rush would be exhilarating. It wasn't the same feeling as the adrenaline rush of a panic attack. It was different. I felt alive. I felt normal.

Normal! That's it! As I raced down that hill, I kept asking myself why I couldn't feel this way all the time? I felt alive. I didn't worry about crashing into trees or wiping out. I honestly felt free for the first time and I was having fun. We did ten or eleven runs that morning before we stopped for something to eat and to brag about what great athletes we all were, *yadda, yadda, yadda.*

But no matter how much fun I was having, the fear and anxiety would always be there lurking in the back of my mind, waiting for its next opportunity to jump out and ruin my day. Just as I was starting to get comfortable with my surroundings and cope with these horrifying lifts, and even have a little fun.

"Hey, let's go try the gondola," one of my buddies said cheerfully.

I thought of a lot of things I wanted to say right then, but of course, I stayed quiet and followed along with the others and got in the 30-yard long line for the gondola trip to the top of the mountain. As we all waited, I tried my best to talk them out of it to no avail, and I quickly resigned myself to the fact that yes, I would have to go through with it.

OK, fine then! Let's all get inside this giant egg-shaped elevator and fly 60 feet off the ground in sub-zero weather. And you'd all better hope we don't stop, because if we do, I plan to throw every damned one of these people off that thing. But hey, yeah, it could be fun.

My anxiety level had never been higher. I counted the giant eggs as they approached the platform -- only twelve to go before I need to get on. The alcohol had started to wear off and I could feel myself starting to go nuts. I thought about how I might be able to fake an injury, or complain that I was about to be sick -- I could tell them it was something I ate, I surmised. Looking back, I should have known I would later become some sort of salesman. When I think about all the relationships I've had in my life including my wife, best friends, the bouncers, the bands, the girls I dated -- everybody -- not one of them ever knew the levels of anxiety I was experiencing. I had developed into a terrific actor.

But now I was looking at my friends who were smiling, relaxed and having a good time, and I wanted to smash them each in the face. I was furious. Why can't I be normal like them? Why can't I just enjoy a day of skiing? I wished I could just snap my fingers and transport myself to the top of a mountain. I would dream about dropping out of a helicopter to ski mountains that no one had ever skied before. But then there was the problem of finding a helicopter... and of course the anxiety about getting inside one.

There were now only two groups remaining in front of us ready to board their gondolas. The attendants split up our group so they could fill each of the giant eggs to their maximum capacity. Noticing this, I dropped back a little. If we were going to be split up, I'd much rather be stuck with a group of people I didn't know; it's less likely these strangers would ever notice something was wrong with me.

The strategy worked perfectly except for one thing. They packed these things like you'd stuff a bunch of jellybeans into a bag. My timing was so good that when the doors opened, I was the first person to enter my giant egg with a crowd of anonymous skiers pushing me from behind.

"Hey you, get to the back of the car," one skier nudged. " We have a lot more people to fit in there."

I was a mess. I retreated to the back of the car and tried to cheat to take up as much space as I could get away with. I fought the urge to bolt back through the door and out to safety, but as I debated the idea in my mind, the door slammed closed. I immediately tried to start a conversation with the man squeezed in next to me, but all he did was smile and nod -- then I noticed he had an ear piece and cassette player. I was boiling. I turned around and opened the small window to revive myself with some fresh air, but someone asked if I would please close it -- little Timmy was chilly.

I wanted to kill them all.

The ride was quick and lasted only about three and a half minutes. But I started to visualize what I would do if it suddenly stopped. We were moving along at a very good rate, but I was still suffering from a major anxiety attack. I could feel the muscles in my stomach knot up and my heart pound. You could see everyone's breath in the cold air, including mine that looked like a fog machine, but suddenly I realized - everything was fine! Remember, the "what ifs" tend to come before the activity. It's not the activity itself that causes the anxiety; it's the thought process about the activity that's the root of the problem. Once I was confident that the gondola would not stop mid-route, and I accepted that it only took a few minutes to reach the mountain top, I knew I would be OK. I knew I could do anything for three and a half minutes. The beast be damned.

Later that night, as we walked back to our cabin from the local bar, we passed the medical center and I noticed it was closed. Next door, the 24-hour food mart was closed too. I said nothing.

I went back to my room and sat on my bed. I didn't sleep a wink that night. My eyes welled with tears and I rocked back and forth wondering why I couldn't be normal like everyone else. I wanted to feel like that guy who was skiing down the hill earlier that morning. I wanted to feel the same exhilaration I'd experienced when riding a minibike or like a baseball player when someone hits a ball right at you. You don't become mired in negative thoughts. You just enjoy. You just do. You just live.

I made sure everyone was in agreement that we had to leave early Sunday morning, making up some excuse that I had to get back. I couldn't get stuck driving in the dark again; I just didn't have the energy for it. And I knew what would happen if I had to drive back late -- my reputation would be ruined. In my mind, I was back in that classroom at St. Mary's.

"Hey guys, guess what! Brian shit his pants. It was hilarious... he was just driving back from the ski trip and he just shit his pants!"

I managed to drive the long road home, out of the woods and back to reality. But what had my reality become?

GUILT

*Guilt is a cancer. Guilt will confine you, torture you, destroy you...
It's a black wall. It's a thief.*

~ **Dave Grohl**

Deep feelings of guilt are a significant part of understanding agoraphobia. Guilt is inescapably connected and serves as a catalyst that deepens and enhances fear and anxiety. And because of this, I exist inside a world where I am able to feel guilty about almost every little thing.

I worked odd jobs throughout my childhood. I remember selling a newspaper called *Grit* where I would make three or four dollars a week. It wasn't much at all, but in my mind, I was contributing something to my family. At six years old, I would fetch the mail for our elderly neighbor Mrs. Hough and she would give me a quarter. My parents had a Superman bank in their bedroom that was about two feet tall, and I watched my dad put his spare change in it every night. When he wasn't around, I would sneak into his bedroom and slip a few of my own quarters through the slot in the top of Superman's head. I don't know if he ever knew.

When I was a little older, I tried to continue to work as much as I could. I worked at the local swim club and I took a part-time job at the local wiener joint. I really liked to work and make money, but more important than that, it helped ease my guilt and made me feel like I was contributing. In my mind, I was pitching in, even though my mom and dad would never consider actually using my money.

In high school, I worked harder, was paid a little more, and was able to save money. I worked every day after school that I didn't have sports and I worked almost every weekend. By then my parents were providing everything we needed as a family more easily, but I still felt an overwhelming urge to pitch in and help. They refused all my money. It broke my heart and my guilt didn't subside; in fact, it grew.

Often the guilt would become so acute that it would create its own panic attack. Other times, the guilt would create a brand of anxiety that would infest my life and feed upon itself for years.

By this time, my father had started his own blow molding company called Luben Plastics. I would help out when I could and learned that I really liked working with my hands on the machines. After high school, I immediately went to work full-time. It wasn't long before Jack, my father's right-hand man and loyal employee who had worked side-by-side with him for many years, suddenly quit. I always believed he saw my arrival as an insult, that he assumed I would be trained to take over the family business one day, destroying his opportunity for advancement. At that point in my life, I had no idea what I was doing: I had never been in business for myself, I couldn't repair any of the complex blow molding machines, and I didn't know the first thing about sales except I knew that the salesmen were the guys who always wore nice suits and drove the fancy cars. But honestly, I couldn't see ever myself driving off to some unknown place to meet with strangers and try to get them to buy something from me. Just the thought itself raised my anxiety to uncomfortable levels.

I always figured I would end up being a shop mechanic. I expected I would learn all about how the blow molding machines operated, I would figure out how to fix them, and then someday I would become the shop supervisor. Of course I had dreams and aspirations of being rich one day, but I had no fathomable idea of how that could possibly happen. Maybe I could invent something, I would think to myself, then people would have to come see me and I could deal with them on my own turf where I felt safe, and I would avoid all the panic and the fear of having to travel to see them. I could keep the Thing caged.

My father may never admit it, but I think he was really angry that Jack left his company the way he did, and subconsciously, he transferred a little of that resentment onto me. We'd argue and I'd finally throw up my hands and ask, "Why didn't I just go to college?"

"You couldn't get into college," both my parents would say.

Despite my lackluster academic performance, I did managed to gain acceptance to URI, where Robbie was going, and the University of Lowell in Massachusetts. But again, the guilt I felt at the prospect of leaving my father alone with his company kept me where I was. It's the George Bailey effect. When Jimmy Stewart's character in the classic film *It's a Wonderful Life* had a chance to go off, see the world and leave Bedford Falls behind, he chose to stay home where he was most needed to run the Bailey Savings & Loan. I could relate to that fictional dilemma because I lived it.

Jack's sudden departure created a lot more work, and my father had to shoulder nearly the entire workload alone. Being the guilt-master I am, I forced myself to work even harder, trying to learn as much as I could as fast as I could. Most, if not all of what happens behind the scenes in a plastics blow molding company, is manual labor, and that was something I could understand and do quickly to become useful. We did not have any of those fancy box making machines in our shop; instead, the boxes all had to be made by hand. I had to set up the box, put the bottles in the box, tape them up, and then stack the boxes on skids. Being in great shape and fresh out of high school, I had a deep reserve of strength and energy, and I dove right in. My usual 9:00 to 5:00 shift become more like 7:30 to 6:30. And in such a competitive industry as plastics, the shop needed to run on a six or seven day week as a 24-hour operation. Every minute that the machines were down and not churning out new bottles, we were losing opportunities to make money.

Jack had been a very good mechanic and supervisor, and I was neither. But I would watch my father diligently, and though we did have fun together at times, most of the time my work life was filled with stress and deepening guilt. My father was a great mechanic in his own right, and had worked on these machines for years, but he didn't know everything about the newer machines he had purchased. The older machines in the shop were breaking down and gradually being replaced by newer models. And though the fancy new machines were more efficient, they included many solid state components that my father had never seen before.

So I took it upon myself to try my best to learn schematics, mechanics, pneumatic pressure on my own -- everything associated with running, operating and maintaining a modern blow molding machine. In my head, I had caused my father's right-hand man and mechanic to quit. I accepted that it was my fault. I had screwed this up. So it was up to me to make sure nothing ever hindered these machines. No one asked me to, but I made it solely my responsibility. This developed my sense of urgency and heightened my anxiety.

I pride myself on being a hard worker. I would always put in extra time and extra effort. Whether it was at the wiener joint, or at a gas station, or delivering newspapers, I always wanted to show that I was the guy who was going to give you that little extra. Maybe it was the guilt that drove me; I didn't want to let anybody down. I wondered sometimes if I even deserved my pay.

There are a thousand things that can go wrong with a blow molding machine, but if you have the right personnel in the right positions, mistakes and breakdowns can be limited. And we, unfortunately, did not. As a new company, we couldn't afford the best help, and many of the employees who worked our second and third shifts just didn't care. They would arrive, go through the motions, put in their time, punch out, and then go home, that is, if they happened to show up at all. As the new supervisor, I would stay in charge until the next supervisor arrived. Some nights, my relief wouldn't show up at all, leaving me stuck in the shop until midnight praying the third shift supervisor would come in. And many times, he didn't.

With all this time on my hands, I trained myself to become the head mechanic. I learned as much as I could on the job, and piled on new responsibilities. Now it was guaranteed that when anything went wrong, my anxiety, panic and guilt levels would ascend to astronomical levels. I would own every screw-up. Things couldn't ever go wrong or I would be letting my family down.

Back then, if I took a rare night off and went out on a date with Robbie, I would carry a beeper. If the beeper went off in the middle of dinner or a movie -- and it frequently did – it meant something was wrong on the machine the supervisor could not fix and we would have to jump in the car and race back to the shop. It would have been easier if I had just called the shop and said I would address it first thing in the morning, but not me. Not *Mr. Guilt.* Instead, I would go to work and leave Robbie sleeping in the car until it was time to take her home.

I felt incredibly guilty doing that to her, it broke my heart, but I felt worse that by not being in the shop when I was needed, I was letting my family down. Then, after I took Robbie home, I would end up returning to the shop to finish up. This was not slave labor. No one was pointing a gun to my head. No one told me to do it. It was my choice. I took it upon myself because the guilt drove me to it.

But I chose this life, and if I didn't like it, there was no one to blame for it but myself. In society today, everybody seems to like to point fingers when something doesn't go their way or they don't get what they want. There was only one direction to point the finger - straight at me. When you finally realize what agoraphobia is all about, you learn it's all up to you. You can choose to get better, or you will slowly sink into its depths.

My father had a top head salesman who was in charge of all our shop's sales. He was cool, good-looking and wore a great suit and had a great car. He had confidence and swagger -- essentially, everything I wanted to have someday. I would pretend to walk around with that swagger, but it was just a show after all. What a joke. Deep down, I had no swagger. I was petrified of everything.

In the early 80's, the salesman started his own blow molding company. Essentially, he could now manufacture his own bottles and sell them to all the great accounts he had established while working for us.

I went crazy. I was absolutely furious! Here he was taking the food right out of my family's mouths. A funny thing about anger fueled by guilt and anxiety -- it starts at level 9!

The moment I heard the news, I ran to my car and said I was going over to his new facility to straighten him out. It was the most angry I had ever been. My father could see the veins popping from my forehead and sensed what I was about to do, and he literally ran into the road and jumped in front of my car to stop me. I nearly ran him over.

It's important to note here that my anger here was two-fold. It wasn't just focused on my belief that he had ripped us off; it was also because I realized what was going to happen next, fear of the inevitable. I would have to be the new salesman. I was too afraid to leave my own room and now I was going to have to learn and endure the whole list of those things that terrified me most. The Thing was back in control and pushing me toward violence.

The next day, I drove over to the guy's facility, got up in his face, and told him in no uncertain terms that if he took another piece of the business from my family, I would break his neck. And I meant it, too. I didn't care about the outcome or ramifications; I was just too incensed.

As you can imagine, over the next several months, our order board became shorter and shorter as our accounts were instead filled by our new competitor, our old salesman. My mother and father pretended not to show it, but I could tell they were nervous about our family future. But my parents have always been able to live in the moment better than me. I lived with anxiety for the future. I could not sleep at night because I was a complete mess, and because I knew they were worried, too. After long sleepless nights and long arguments with the beast, I decided I had to try it. I had to try to learn how to become a salesman. The guilt was driving me again. And I would endure it all without telling anybody.

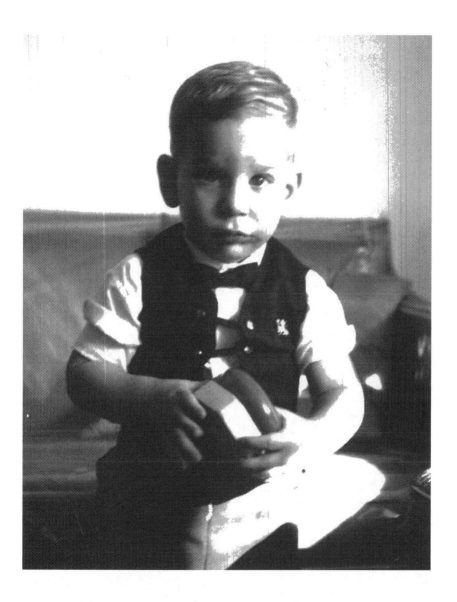

Growing up in New Jersey. Even at this young age,
I was in tune with my anxiety and fear.
Photo Courtesy: **Brian Beneduce**

Kindergarten at St. Mary's where I suffered my
first panic attack in front of my classmates
Photo Courtesy: **Brian Beneduce**

I was lucky enough to marry my high school sweetheart
and best-friend. Robbie has been my rock
and I made a mistake by trying to hide my panic
disorder from her during our decades of marriage.
Photo Courtesy: **Brian Beneduce**

I was all smiles in this photo but the torture I felt just traveling

to our honeymoon still frightens me all these years later

Photo Courtesy: **Brian Beneduce**

To manage my disorder, I exercise both mentally and physically.
It's the only way that I can keep the beast at bay.

Photo Courtesy: **Brian Beneduce**

Conquering my fear meant challenging myself in new ways.
I never thought I could captain my own boat, but I did it.
Photo Courtesy: **Brian Beneduce**

I coached my son Michael in youth baseball and I am
proud of the player and the person he has become.
Photo Courtesy: **Brian Beneduce**

When I watched my daughter Jenn play soccer, I'd always place my hand over my chest to let her know that she always gave 110 percent and played with heart.
Photo Courtesy: **Brian Beneduce**

Despite my struggles, I have all I need in life. I have a great family and a great business. I still battle the Thing but I now understand that I am not fighting alone. My family is by my side.

7

THE BRIDGE

*Pleased to meet you, Hope you guess my name But
what's puzzling you, Is the nature of my game!*
~ **The Rolling Stones**, *Sympathy for the Devil*

My family business was failing, and here I was, too handcuffed
by anxiety and fear to walk into someone's office and ask for a
simple order that would save the company.

The voices in my head were never more at odds – The
Thing was telling me I was worthless and needed to turn around
and go back home, while my good ego was urging me to charge
into that prospective client's office and fight for my family. My
problem was never convincing a customer to place the order; it
was about just being able to get myself in front of that customer
in the first place.

The beast had been slowly coiling around its prey since my childhood. Now it was poised to squeeze me and swallow me whole.

It was the eve of the most critical business meeting of my life to that point and sleep was impossible. I tossed and turned as Robbie slept serenely beside me, oblivious to the fact that the strong, proud man who was lying beside her was lost in a funnel cloud of fear.

"Please fall asleep. Stop worrying," I begged myself,

I planned to leave just after five the next morning, determined to beat the infamous rush hour traffic that collected along Interstate 95 every morning from southern Connecticut through New York. My destination was just beyond the George Washington Bridge in Secaucus, New Jersey.

And here it was now already 1:30 a.m., and I only had a few hours before I had to get up, shower, put on my suit, grab my briefcase and pretend everything was just great. But the creature had taken flight in my mind.

"*What if you hit traffic anyway? What if you lose control of yourself or your car and crash into someone?*" hissed the beast. "*What if you completely lose it this time, your throat closes and you pass out on the road?*"

"Go to sleep," I told myself. "*You know where every blue hospital sign is located across the entire state of Connecticut. Everything will be fine.*"

The Thing was undeterred.

But what if you make it to the meeting, and they want you to speak to more than three or four people? What if you have a panic attack during the meeting? What if you can't think of an excuse? So what if you just call and cancel then? You could just tell them you're sick... and Robbie will believe that, too, since she knows the kind of workaholic you are. You're always run down.

I left that morning even earlier than I planned to see how many exits I could pass before the anxiety became so intense that it would force me to get off the interstate at one of those blue hospital signs. Sometimes I had even run my truck into a pole, crashed it, just to avoid the inevitable.

As I traveled farther south, I knew traffic would get worse. It always does. Many people who live in southern Connecticut work in Manhattan and get up very early themselves to fight through the awful, chronic congestion of vehicles.

About an hour and a half into my trip, I reached the first tollbooth. My anxiety rose as I knew there is no way to get off and also that there wouldn't be any help available once I got stuck in one of those toll lines. But I gritted my teeth and breezed through this toll quickly.

I tuned the radio to New York's WFAN knowing they start the daily traffic reports at 6 a.m. I prayed they wouldn't report a stoppage on the George Washington Bridge -- the only logical connection to Secaucus from where I was.

As I passed through the city of Stamford, Connecticut, I started to see red brake lights ahead of me. Traffic was slowing. Farther ahead, I could see dozens of those red lights stretching out for what appeared to be miles. Red lights meant that I was trapped. The Thing knew there was now nowhere to get off the highway, nowhere to get help, and nowhere to hide. I felt my heart pounding. My anxiety level instantly shot from 3 to 5.

I started to weave in and out of the lanes the best I could to avoid actually stopping my truck. Above me was a huge green highway sign pointing me toward the George Washington Bridge. I forced myself to follow it. Now there really was no turning back. My anxiety level rose to 6. I held my breath and continued forward as best I could.

The radio station reported that a tractor-trailer had overturned about a mile before the bridge and that cars had now completely stopped. I was sitting on the Bruckner Expressway on an overpass that felt like it was ten thousand feet off the ground. Everyone around me was annoyed at the traffic, but I was crawling out of my skin. My anxiety rose to level 7.

As the morning wore on, the air temperature on that muggy July day increased. The engine in my little Toyota pickup only had four cylinders and I could hear it straining and sputtering. I quickly switched off the air conditioning as I couldn't let it overheat out here a thousand feet in the air with nowhere to go. The suit I wore -- the only suit I owned -- was made from a thick, warm woolen material designed for winter weather, and now I was sweating right through it.

Traffic was barely creeping along, and the lanes were shrinking from six to four to two to one. I realized none of these jerks was going to let me in. My front bumper came within an inch of the car in the lane next to me, and the driver flipped me off. I swore, screamed and flipped him off right back. I needed that human interaction so badly I was willing to get out and fight him, if necessary. The beast was growing inside me once again.

The burst of anger was welcome, but unfortunately, provided only temporary relief.

I had now successfully crossed the Bruckner Expressway and the massive George Washington Bridge ahead remained my final obstacle. I had timed it perfectly. But the radio report now informed us that the accident had caused about a twenty-minute delay. My heart felt as if it was ready to burst from my chest, and I was drenched in sweat. My tie, which I loosened several miles back, felt as if it's re-tightening around my neck on its own. The Thing was constricting, squeezing.

I desperately tried to continue breathing and not pass out. My fists were pounding on the steering wheel. I was rapidly approaching level 8 panic attack. Two more levels and I'd be dead.

My truck inched along as I finally reached the foot of the bridge. My throat was closing even more. Pretending that everything was okay; I glanced over at the driver in the car next to me and smiled. I must have looked like a complete psychopath

The worst part of any bridge is the middle. At that point, there is no going back and nowhere to get off except to plunge over the railing.

"Is that what you want to do?" The Thing asked me. *"Do you want to end this torment once and for all?"*

I didn't know what to do. Every part of my body was shaking. I glanced down at the briefcase on the seat next to me and realized this is the easiest part of my day -- I still had that big meeting at to attend. Halfway over the bridge, I pulled out my meeting notes and started to shuffle through them, trying to concentrate on the words written on the pages and not the bridge. I begged my truck to not overheat. I looked down again at my notes and they looked like scribbles. My vision blurred and I didn't even recognize the words I was reading.

I tried switching the radio to a music channel, then panicked when I realized that the station didn't offer traffic updates. I started spinning the knobs, momentarily forgetting how the radio worked and couldn't find WFAN. I had AM and FM mixed up. I was eating up time with these ridiculous distractions, until I discovered that I was three quarters of the way over the bridge. Ahead of me the red lights were starting to disappear and traffic is moving along slowly. My anxiety level dropped down to 7, then 6, then 5. I started to feel human again. I felt the muscles in my throat ease and reached for a bottle of water. I tried to drink, but I still couldn't swallow, and then I feared I'd choke and drown. I thought to myself:

"What the hell is wrong with me? Why can't I even drink a damn bottle of water?" I asked myself. "Why am I going crazy like this?"

People who suffer from anxiety and panic attacks feel and see things that others simply do not. There are hundreds of bridges and obstacles that normal people cross every day which they don't see. But I see them all.

As I neared my Secaucus exit, having survived the George Washington Bridge, I began to drive over some other ordinary and anonymous bridge that was about two miles long and spanned one of New Jersey's many crossways below when I suddenly heard something. My engine had overheated. The truck had started to slow.

"Oh dear God! Please, no! This can't be happening! Not now! No!" I screamed aloud. "Please, please, please let me get to the top so I can at least coast down the other side."

It was my worst fear. I was exactly halfway across this bridge, at the very top, and the truck had quit.

I screamed again. I started to cry. Though no one could see or hear me. I pounded on the steering wheel. I was petrified. I could feel the Thing wrapping itself tightly around my entire body.

"*Run,*" it told me.

I got out of the truck, leaving it parked in the right travel lane blocking everyone behind me. Drivers all sat on their horns, waved angry fists and cursed me. I was frantic and didn't give a damn.

The soles of my best dress shoes slammed against the deck of the bridge rapid fire, first right then left as fast as I could move them, creating an eerie echo matched only by my heart pounding with fury in my chest. My hands were clenched in fists so tight my knuckles were turning blue, and my arms pumped franticly like one of the blow molding machines back in our shop. My necktie was stretched back over my shoulder and stood straight out behind me, and the flaps of my suit jacket flailed and fluttered so fast I looked like some type of bird trying to take flight. Hot car exhaust stung my lungs with each inhale, but no matter how uncomfortable, I would not allow it to slow me down.

If I didn't get off this bridge right now, I knew I was going to die.

Dozens of drivers in a confused daze watched me, a 5-foot 10-inch man in a white dress shirt and tie, sprint past them. I was humiliated by what I thought they were thinking of me. But it did not matter. I had no choice.

When I reached the bottom of the bridge, my shirt was saturated with sweat and my trousers were twisted almost sideways. My hair had matted against my forehead and my cheeks were candy apple red. As I hyperventilated, I looked ahead for a refuge -- some kind of oasis -- where I could stop to try to relax and regain my composure. But ahead, there was nothing but a sea of cars, perhaps a thousand of them, and miles of guardrails and grey highway. I scratched at my face in frustration and terror.

Suddenly, one of the cars came to life in a flash of blue spinning lights. It was a police cruiser and it had worked its way to the breakdown lane to ease up alongside me. I could read the concern in the officer's squinting eyes as he peered at me through his open window. I was a complete mess. He had to assume I was being chased by some deranged psychopath, a terrorist, or some rabid wild animal. I was so engulfed in fear I could not speak. He spoke first.

"Are you OK, sir?"

A thousand thoughts ricocheted around inside my skull all at once. I was sure the officer could hear my heart pounding, or even see it pulsating beneath my white dress shirt. I could not let him see how upset I was. As the officer emerged from his car, I noticed the fingers of his right hand were slowly wrapping around the handle of his service revolver. I realized he could not possibly know what he was walking into.

"Everything is fine. Thank you," I panted.

"Then why are you running?"

"Oh... it's because of my pickup truck.... It broke down on top of the bridge... I was on my way to get help... maybe a tow." I tried frantically to catch my breath and sound intelligent, but every word I managed to utter was a struggle.

I assume he thought I was sick, because he kept asking if I was sure I was OK.

There is one phrase you should never say to anyone suffering a severe anxiety and panic attack, and that is, *"Are you OK."* It is an indication that the person notices and acknowledges that there is something terribly wrong, and it drives the anxiety up to astronomical levels. *"Relax, you'll be OK,"* is another. If I could relax, would I be acting like this? It makes the thoughts in your head swirl until you go insane.

The stone-faced officer acted like he didn't quite believe me, sighed, then waved me into the back seat of his patrol car.

For the briefest of moments, I felt liberated. Help was here. Thank God.

"You need to stay with your vehicle until a tow truck can take you off the turnpike, the officer informed me.

A rush of pure, hot adrenaline swept back through my body. I felt my red cheeks go pale. My throat closed again. I couldn't breathe -- it was a feeling of pure dread. I believed I was going to die. He was taking me back to the top of the bridge. Puzzled, he stared at me through his rearview mirror.

"Are you sure you are alright?"

"I'm just light-headed... from all the running... that's all... I'll be fine... in a few minutes." Then I lied again and told him I had the flu.

"If you're sick, why didn't you stay home?" he asked.

"I have this very important meeting with one of a big customer in Secaucus."

"Well then, you'd better clean yourself up. You look like shit."

How could a tough guy like me explain that I was weak, that I didn't know what was wrong with me, that I was so afraid of being on that bridge that I was running away so I wouldn't jump to my death?

How could I explain the Thing?

The patrol car was pointing in the wrong direction, so it needed to leave the bridge, take an exit, U-turn, then head back over in the other direction, U-turn again, then drop me at my truck. It was the longest two mile drive of my life, and as each second ticked by, my chest grew tighter, and my hands trembled faster. I didn't think it possible that my level of terror and anxiety could rise beyond what I had already experienced that morning. But the fear was getting worse. I was at level 9 -- no doubt about it. The beast moved in for the kill.

Once back at the top, the officer let me out of the car and pointed at the ground.

"Now stay here until the tow arrives."

"OK, I promise. I will," I lied again.

As his car disappeared below the crest, my panic peaked. I felt a powerful impulse to jump off the bridge. I fought it. I fought this suicidal urge with everything in my being.

I was in control of how I lived and at least for now, how I would die.

Instead of running north like I had done the first time, this time I decided to simply run south. It didn't matter what the officer had told me, I needed to get off that bridge -- *immediately.*

The terror and panic that rolled in waves through my body was taking its toll, and exhaustion and paranoia were setting in. I started to see police cars everywhere -- dozens of them -- at least that was what I thought. Perhaps I was hallucinating. But before long, the lights from a second, very real New Jersey State Police car were flashing in front of me, and another officer was walking in my direction.

By now I was sure I looked like I was completely out of my mind. And if he thought that, too, he would have been right. I couldn't have blamed him if he had pulled his revolver, or even shot at me.

It's what the Thing wanted.

But I was fortunate that the officer remained professionally calm, and we walked through the same conversation I had already had with his colleague. And he also insisted that I had to remain with my vehicle.

"And what if I don't?" I asked frantically.

"Lock me up, I don't care," I thought.

"You need to either stay with your truck, or you will have to come with me to the station house," he insisted.

"I'm sick, sir. You can take me back to my truck if you want to, but I am not going to stay on top of that bridge!"

I was placed in the back of the squad car and driven to the Secaucus, New Jersey State Police Barracks. I didn't care about my business appointment anymore; in fact, I don't think I cared about anything. But I was grateful. I was drenched in sweat and felt sick and I knew if I passed out there, the officers would simply rush me to the nearest hospital. I started to feel safer. I began to calm down.

At the station, I told them I was just a businessman with a fear of heights. I said I simply couldn't stay on top of a bridge.

It was the biggest lie of all. I wasn't afraid of heights -- I was afraid of everything!

BLOOD &
SWEAT

"There's one thing I want you to do for me, win. WIN!"
— **Adrian Balboa**, *Rocky II*

The Thing had me on the ropes, pummeling my body and mind with two giant fists packed with panic and fear. Our family business went under and we began to sell off our assets. Once again, I blamed myself for the shame it brought on my mom and dad. But now I was growing a family of my own and I needed to find some way to control this severe disorder before hurling myself off that next bridge and losing it all.

Robbie and I had been married for five years and we were expecting our first child. I felt that if I couldn't save my dad's company, I would make damn sure that I would be able to provide for my wife and child, whatever the cost.

I had to look deep within myself. I had to stare straight into the eyes of the beast. My anxiety had always been brought on by my fear of the inevitable. The dreaded *What ifs?*

Each time I felt the Thing creeping toward me, my body and mind would tighten and I would immediately try to resist. I would unsheathe my proverbial sword and try to slay the beast at the mouth of its cave. I would expend all my energy trading blow for blow until I was completely exhausted and most vulnerable to the terrifying impulses that were designed to kill me. I simply could not survive another day unless I altered my strategy and discovered a proper coping mechanism. I needed to get healthy in both body and mind. But first, I needed inspiration. I've always been a champion of the underdog, as I consider myself the ultimate underdog for what I've had to endure and overcome in life.

"I will become the hero of my own story, not the victim," I told myself. "And every hero needs a theme song."

I grabbed my portable tape player and popped in a favorite cassette of mine. I then closed my eyes and listened. The sound of a high note trumpet traveled through my headphones and my heart began to race. I could feel Bill Conti's rousing orchestral score for *Rocky* hitting every one of my nerve endings. As the classic movie theme continued to play, I visualized myself in the Sylvester Stallone role, hitting the heavy bag, chopping wood and racing up the tall steps of the Philadelphia Museum of Art.

Rocky's strength was underscored by the way he could take a beating in the ring before mounting a miraculous comeback. I understood this and then sought other examples to help me create my own strategy. In the real-life ring, Muhammad Ali managed to out think and outlast a much younger, stronger George Foreman before scoring a stunning knockout in the so-called "Rumble in the Jungle" in Zaire, Africa in 1974.

Ali stayed pinned against the ropes for seven grueling rounds as Foreman landed devastating punch after devastating punch, until the younger fighter was so exhausted that he could no longer lift his arms. When the bell rang for the eighth round, Ali pounced on poor George and sent him crashing to the canvas. He called the strategy; "Rope-a-Dope". I analyzed this fight and said, "Aha". This was it! Instead of battling the beast toe-to-toe, I would welcome the onslaught of fear and panic and let it wash over me until the Thing had nothing left in its arsenal. At that moment, I would pounce, just like Ali and my fictional hero Rocky Balboa had done. But I'd need to increase both my stamina and my power if I was to be successful. If I was to survive. If I was to win.

I began training even harder at the gym, as if I was about to fight for the heavyweight championship of the world. Boxing isn't my thing, but powerlifting is. I've had a passion for it ever since I picked up that booklet as a kid. With powerlifting, it's you against the weight. Unlike bodybuilding where you work out and build muscle only to be judged by other people, the strategy behind powerlifting is more objective: lift heavy, eat more, get bigger, and repeat.

For a severe agoraphobic like me, I needed a routine that was both healthy and meaningful. As I've said, the gym had become my fortress; my sanctuary to prepare for the next battle with the Thing, whenever it would come. Every time I'd suffered a severe panic attack, I'd immediately lose control of my breathing, which would lead to dizziness and even hallucinations. Powerlifting taught me how to control my breaths, accept the massive amount of weight on my chest or on the canvas, channel my energy and lift.

I became an accomplished powerlifter and even owned and operated my own gym for a time. And while I enjoyed the camaraderie and lifestyle, I knew that I had to get back to the business world to provide a better future for my family and to show the Thing that no bridge was going to stand in the way of my success.

The road would be both difficult and rewarding. Over the years, while battling the beast, I've been able to build a plastics packaging company from scratch that turned ten and fifteen cent items into over $20 million in sales. We're not selling $250,000 Lamborghinis or $3 million yachts here either, we've achieved our success -- *literally* -- fifteen cents at a time.

It took more than a decade of getting my brains beaten and my ego shattered while trying to get my foot in the door of customers who did not want to see me, and all the while, dealing with horrible bouts of anxiety and panic.

"Go ahead beast, punch yourself out," I'd say while sitting in my car, waiting for the torture to subside.

Now, instead of running away from my disorder, or committing some manic act, I focused on my breathing, listened to the Rocky theme on my cassette player and pumped myself up for the challenge ahead.

"You just tamed the Thing," I'd remind myself. "Now go in there and win that business."

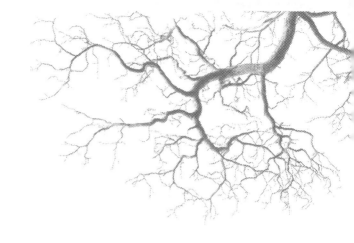

MY TOOLBOX

We all have rituals that we perform to give us the proper focus needed to tackle whatever challenges that lay ahead. Hall of Fame third baseman Wade Boggs ate chicken before every game. Tennis star Rafael Nadal takes a shower 45 minutes before every match. And I listen to the Rocky theme before every big meeting.

But as a severe agoraphobic, I can't rely on superstitions alone. I need to bring more artillery onto the battlefield each time I face the Thing. My weapon is my toolbox and inside are the mental instruments I use to control my inner fear so that I can accomplish my daily tasks. I call it my "toolbox" because I'm a mechanic by trade and only a salesman by necessity. When I speak to groups of children about anxiety, I have them close their eyes and imagine a magical backpack that holds all the utensils they would need to ease their minds whenever they are scared.

Inside my mental toolbox is a list of all the things I do not want. It's easy to write down on paper or in your mind all the things that you'd like to have – better health, fame, power, love. But how can you achieve something if you never consider the consequences of not having it. I don't want to be alone. Therefore, I work extra hard to improve my relationship with my wife Robbie, our kids, those who work for me and anyone else that I care about. I don't want to be in debt, so I work to make sure that I never extend myself or my business. And finally, I don't want to be afraid all the time.

Now this is a little more complicated. It's diametrically opposed to the Thing's wants and needs. I combat this by being happy for no reason. I laugh and sing every single day because it fills me with positive energy and that energy serves as kryptonite for the beast.

I also take out the garbage. Now garbage can weigh down your toolbox if you don't take it out several times a day. By that I mean, I no longer get angry about things I cannot control. I used to scream at my radio when I heard a sports debate I didn't agree with.

"Brian, the radio is not listening to you," I would have to remind myself.

I stopped getting angry and started getting involved in whatever cause I believed in because mobilization and commitment are the only true ways to create change.

I began visualizing the promise of each day. What could I accomplish over the next 24 hours? Who can I help? The Thing absolutely hates this. It feeds and sustains itself on self doubt and worry. Excitement and confidence can keep the beast in its cave.

I refuse to blame others for my mistakes. It's always easy to find a scapegoat or boogie man to point the finger at when you face trouble. A fixed personality is a myth. We are all adaptable. We can all change. I own each mistake and use it as a platform to fix the problem. As a mechanic, I can fix anything so I think of my body and mind as a machine.

I place my tool box directly in front of the cave where the Thing shelters in darkness until it can smell my fear. Above this cave is where I visualize a large tree, one I call my anxiety tree whose branches and roots hold the negative, painful feelings that we all face, whether we are agoraphobic or not. The branches represent fear of getting ill, a fear of flying, the idea that we are not worthy or that we might embarrass ourselves. Digging into the ground below the surface and into the beast's cave are the roots to our neuroses; anxiety, terror, fear, panic and ultimately depression.

When I flew alone for the first time, I carried my imaginary toolbox with me. After buckling in for the long flight ahead, I reached down and pulled out a list of inspirational quotes that I had memorized. While others ordered wine, beer and cocktails to keep them from losing their nerve at 30,000 feet, I chanted silently until the Thing could not bear it any longer and left me alone. I also reflected back on all those fearful bridges, tunnels, elevators, and sales meetings and asked myself, what really happened there?

The situations didn't cause the panic. I did not have the crippling physical feelings first. The feelings were manufactured in my head and caused the anxiety only after I had been thinking about them. I came to understand that I had been given a ticket to ride no matter what. I climbed onto the roller coaster knowing what to expect – a few minutes of sheer terror followed by relief and tranquility. All I needed to do was brace myself and wait for the harrowing ride to end.

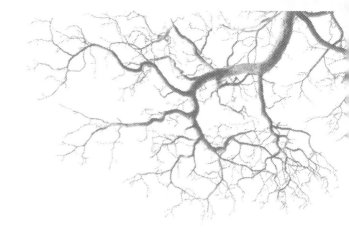

10

THE BUSINESS CONFERENCE

There are nights when the wolves are
silent and only the moon howls.

~ **George Carlin**

There are certain words you should never use around someone who has agoraphobia, and they include *vacation, trip, journey,* and *travel*. The mere mention of these words can send them into a fit of terror.

Traveling means that you have to abandon your safe place and leave behind everything that you know and also those things that keep your anxiety in check and the Thing tucked securely in its cave.

As a businessman, the only other word I can think of that might be worse than *trip* is *conference.*

I have missed out on countless business trips over the years due to my severe disorder. I always tried to make excuses, create an illness or flat-out lie to avoid any kind of travel. But there were also those times when there was nothing I could do. I had to take the trip -- *I had to do it anyway.*

In the plastics industry, I made my reputation as a middleman connecting vendors who manufacture the product with new customers who need it. It may sound counterproductive, but in this business, vendors are always more important than customers. I believed with a little hustle, I could always find a new customer, but there really are only a limited number of important vendors. After all, without product, there is no business anyway.

When I first started my company, the stress that accompanied keeping our vendors happy was extreme. Early on, I was lucky to become friendly with a large bottle cap company in New Jersey. I did everything I could to grow our business relationship. As I successfully formed this bond, the vendor rewarded me with an invitation to one of its major conferences in Vermont where we'd talk business and hit the powdery ski slopes.

This was my second invitation; I had come up with an excuse not to attend the year before. But now this vendor had become even more important to my bottom line and was supplying eleven of my best customers. I couldn't say no again or do anything that might insult them. I could not risk jeopardizing our relationship.

My contact with this vendor was their sales manager. He was a complete jerk and well-known to treat people like shit. But I needed him, and I was able to get into his good graces so well that he invited me along on this wonderful trip. Other invitees included over 120 other people who were also their customers. And because I was a bottle distributor, they wanted me there badly -- we were in short supply. I knew they needed me to be there, but I couldn't let on that I needed them more.

The resort was only about five hours from my office, so like most agoraphobics; I left my office early in the morning to ensure I would arrive safely several hours early. I could not deal with the idea of getting lost, and I absolutely couldn't handle driving alone after dark. I was the first to arrive at the resort and too early to check into my room. So what do you do when you're in Vermont with nothing else to do? You drive around until you find the nearest hospital, of course. And I found it eight miles away.

My challenge that weekend was compounded by the fact that I had to tame the beast while also trying to impress an important vendor.

What made it even worse was that nine of my regular customers were going to be there, too. This conference had rapidly developed into an agoraphobic's worst nightmare.

We all stayed in a series of cabins that most people would consider quite charming, but I considered complete hell. There were no televisions or radios. I also learned that each of these small cabins would house twelve of us. I found it strange that I'd be sharing a bathroom with a dozen people I didn't even know.

Moreover, I was terrified by the possibility that my business bunkmates might witness me devolve into a full blown panic attack. I had kept the beast a secret from my family and friends. Robbie, my wife and best friend, didn't even know how sick I was. That's because I swallowed the feelings of intense anxiety as best I could when others were around. This was not a healthy way of addressing the problem, as I lied to my loved ones and lied to myself.

The guest list for the conference included several high-profile executives running public companies, CEO's, and CFO's. In fact, they could all potentially become new customers of mine someday.

And of course there was me, the owner of a company called Ocean State Packaging, a guy scared to leave his house, scared to ride a ski lift, and scared of just about everything. I had to act like nothing was bothering me, while at the same time, convince the big shots that I belonged there. To a salesperson, it was a veritable buffet of new business. I was fishing in a freshly stocked pond. But my only goal was to simply make it through the first night.

After we all took our turns introducing ourselves, each one of us was asked to make a brief speech. I slipped out of the room to fake a phone call so I would not have attention thrust upon me. Again, I felt like I was back at St. Mary's struggling to hold my bowels.

The organizer suggested that we all retire early for the night because we had to be at the ski mountain first thing in the morning.

The last thing in the world I wanted to do was go to bed early. I did not want to be in a strange place with strange people with just my thoughts to guide me. The Thing had awakened and was ready to seize upon me once more.

Thank goodness we each had separate rooms in the cabin, although the walls were thin.

The only good thing about my room was it was full of books. I had never heard of most of the titles, but the selection included a copy of *Moby Dick*. It didn't take long before I could hear snoring through the thin cabin wall behind me. How dare they sleep! Just like on the gondola, and on the airplane, I hated them. I despised *normal* people. These guys were pulling in salaries in the hundreds of thousands of dollars, having a good time, and I hated them all. I opened *Moby Dick* to a random chapter and started to read. I read the same chapter at least a dozen times. It was the chapter where writer Herman Melvillle described Captain Ahab's whalebone leg and how the captain blamed the intense pain it caused him on the elusive white whale – *Moby Dick*. As I scoured the pages again and again, I found myself identifying with the revenge prone sea captain. My white whale was the Thing. No matter how many times that I tried to harpoon the monster and kill it once and for all, it always appeared to be just out of my grasp.

I finally closed the book and closed by eyes.

"I'm going to figure this out, I told myself. "I am not going to go insane here. I am going to work through this. I will not go mad"

When you're getting ready to exercise, or getting ready to fight, there is an adrenaline rush. There is a moment when you realize that the battle is you against you -- some refer to this as "the fight within you." I have always had an aggressive side to me, which was borne from my need to protect myself.

It's at night when the Thing is at its strongest, fueled by my panic and fear. Every time I tried to fight it, the bad thought process would reboot itself and start all over again. The tentacles of fear and doubt grow, become more powerful, and try to drive me insane. The Thing was vicious, but now I had my own harpoon. I dove into my imaginary toolbox and went to work, luring the giant beast out, lulling it before finally applying my methods of visualization – How I was going to win those big shots over the next day, inspirational quotes and finally – the Rocky theme. I rope-a-doped the beast and then counter attacked with positive thoughts until it was punch drunk and staggering back to its stool, at least for now.

"Yo Adrian, I did it!" I muttered to myself as I finally drifted off for a few short hours of sleep.

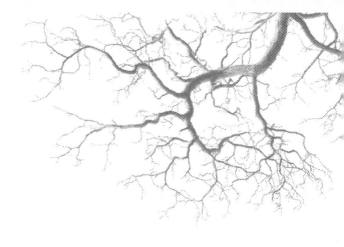

WHERE
ANXIETY
LIVES

*"Life is like a roller coaster. You can either scream
every time there is a bump or you can throw your
hands in the air and enjoy the ride."*
— Anonymous

I've described through the chapters of this book where severe
anxiety resides in my subconscious mind. I have painted a dark,
foreboding place where the Thing serves as gate keeper, tormentor
and potential executioner.

In the physical world, anxiety can be found in crowded places, it can be found in an aircraft traveling at 20,000 feet and it can be found in places that are designed to make you happy.

My first vacation on a real cruise ship brought me all sorts of stress and anxiety. While other passengers including my wife were eager to check out the pool, the casino deck and the restaurant, I immediately wandered off in search of the ship's infirmary. It appeared to be a clean office with all the latest medical technology, but one visit did not quell my growing fear.

That evening, after dinner on the ship, I feigned a bad headache so I could visit the medical staff and interrogate them, all the while scanning their faces for reactions to my questioning.

"What happens if someone gets really sick?" I asked. "What if someone has a heart attack? How do you get them safely off the ship? Does the Coast Guard come and get you?"

The staff assured me that they had the proper training and emergency protocols in place for just about every health scenario I could think of. They didn't realize the extent of my imagination and that my list of possible emergency situations was infinite.

I had remembered to pack my bathing suit, sunscreen and a sport coat for a formal dinner but the most important thing that I kept on me at all times was my imaginary toolbox, which I had used over and over again until we were safely off the ship and back home.

Family friendly destinations such as Walt Disney World instill nothing but fear in me. When I traveled to the so-called "Happiest Place on Earth" with Robbie and my young children, Jennifer and now Michael, I felt like one of those costumed characters dancing, smiling and posing for pictures. On the outside, I was laughing and enjoying myself, but inside the costume, I was sweating and looking for a way out.

I had kept the beast in check for most of the trip as we made our way through the Magic Kingdom and some other Disney theme parks. I was laser focused on making sure that my little ones were happy and that I was helping my wife with all the things young families lug around; strollers, stuffed animals and sippy cups. I had no time in my day to deal with the beast. It's as if I hung a sign at the mouth of its cave – *Gone Fishin'*.

"If I can just make it one more day," I told myself. "We'll be on our way home from Orlando and I'll be back in my safe place."

I should not have said the word "If". That word is a proverbial question mark and it's not the proper use of visualization.

What I should have said was; "I'm gonna make it today and it's all gonna be great!"

This positive approach might have kept the beast from breaching the gates of the Magic Kingdom; instead slithered its way in, crawled up my back and into my brain just as we entered Epcot. At that moment, my entire body tightened and my sunburned face drew stark white.

I told Robbie that the sun was getting to me and that I just needed a minute. While my wife disappeared with the kids in one of those long maze lines for the latest kiddie ride, I began frantically searching for a way out.

I was running around like a madman, the Thing was now controlling my arms and legs. I was no longer in control as it had me in its vice like grip. Disney security guards were quickly alerted to my erratic behavior and deemed me an immediate threat. They approached me and sternly asked me to come with them.

"I just gotta get outta here," I pleaded. "I'm not on drugs, I'm not violent. I'm having a major panic attack."

They marched toward what I can only describe as "Disney jail", watched and waited for me to slowly bring my anxiety level down from a 9, to a 7, and finally a two. I regained my composure and apologized for the embarrassing situation.

When my kids were young, I loved and hated taking them to the zoo. Zoos are designed with a maze of paths that all seem to lead to snack bars and gift shops, but almost never to medical help or the exits. I would be holding my kids by the hands following these confusing paths wondering;

What's the fastest way out of here? What if I pass out and hit my head? My kids are so small; will they know what to do?

What if... What if... What if...

I was programmed to despise the word "vacation." I would become physically ill days before we'd be ready to leave to go anywhere. For days, my mind would roll through a list of all my sources of anxiety -- the flight, the cruise ship, an island hideaway, a hotel with elevators, nearby hospitals. Simply coping with vacation became a full-time activity.

Sometimes in the middle of the night while in some exotic locale, I'd crawl out of bed and call down to the front desk of the hotel just to make sure somebody would be there to answer. And fearing that I would suffer a full-fledged panic attack and not make it to the elevator, I would always ask for a room on the lower floors and then proceed to map out all the staircases and exits.

It is these little things that tend to bother me the most because in the mind of an agoraphobic, you're continually wondering how you could possibly handle all the big important things in life if you are distracted by all these little ones. If anxiety and panic are the roots of a tree, the deeper those roots will extend into the fertile recesses of your mind if you allow them to go unchecked.

When you rely on positive reinforcement in questionable situations, you can declaw and muzzle the beast while avoiding embarrassment for you and your loved ones and simply enjoy the ride.

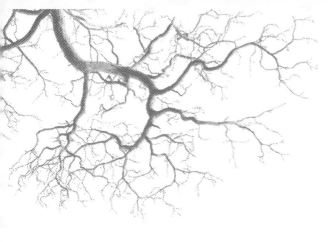

THE TEST

There are no limits.
There are only plateaus, and you must not
stay there. You must go beyond them.
~ **Bruce Lee**

My business was booming. I had clients, I had vendors, I had cash flow, but I still had severe anxiety and panic attacks and a growing urge to never leave my house ever again. My success wasn't helping my condition.

"You're making ten times more than what you made as a mechanic," I told myself. "It's time to rest, take a break and enjoy life. You don't have to do this anymore."

But then there was that other voice. There is a scene in *Rocky* where he's is lying on a bed talking to his young son. His son asks if he ever feels fear when he fights one of those big, monster-like guys.

"Yeah, I do," Rocky answers in that deep throaty Stallone voice. "But then there's that other voice in my head that says I can take the punishment, I can take the fight, I can take the hits, and I can keep going."

Today, I am 58 years-old and I have built a multi-million dollar company. But I didn't do it alone. I'm proud to say there are many people, both real and imagined that have provided inspiration to my life. Rocky is a perfect example of this. We all have that inner superhero, that Batman, Superman or Wonder Woman who represents the best version of ourselves. The most enduring fictional characters are always fighting something deep within themselves while also battling evil external forces that are hell bent on destroying a city or the universe.

Like many of these characters, I can't pretend to be normal and just sweep the anxiety and panic under the carpet. The Thing was too powerful. It never sleeps, and yet I always felt compelled to keep going, and to keep fighting for my family and my business.

I saw what happened to my parents when their business was taken away from them. I lived it right along with them. That particular fear always follows me, and has helped fertilize the roots of my anxiety tree, helping it drill deeper. In the back of my mind, there's nothing there to stop it except my own will and my buddy Danny's voice yelling at me, insisting I keep fighting.

Danny was the kid I had fought in the end zone back in high school. Surprisingly, we became the best of friends and remain so to this day. We're as close as brothers.

Danny is probably the toughest guy I have ever known. We became weightlifting partners and I can say without a doubt that Danny has made me both mentally and physically stronger than I could ever have been training by myself; he brought out the lion in me. Although it's OK to push yourself through anxiety and panic attacks in the gym, you can't get away with that in real life.

On business trips, I would call Danny from my hotel room in the middle of a panic attack. I would be a total mess. I remember *The Tonight Show with Johnny Carson* would be going off the air and I knew I would have to shut off the lights at some point. I'd call Danny at home and he would talk me through the moment in a very soft-spoken but tough way. He was sort of like that trainer in the corner every boxer hopes for:

The words and phrases he used are the same ones I would repeat in my own mind for years to come during the worst attacks, when the beast was trying to kill me.

But looking back on it now, I've learned it's exactly what you must *not* do. I didn't realize then that you can't fight anxiety, because it feeds on the same flash of adrenaline you need to fight it. It's not like facing the bullies of the world.

The scary thoughts I needed to fight were evolving deep inside my own mind and would get worse when I closed my eyes. I would rather lose a dozen physical fights with anyone than be forced to fight against the incredible scary and terrifying sensations the human body is capable of producing.

If I did that, the Thing would win for sure. That's when I learned to rope-a-dope the beast.

As my kids grew up, I explained my tool box method to them, comparing it to a backpack.

I would urge them to stuff their own coping methods in their backpacks because you never know when you're going to need it. Feel the fear, and do it anyway... *and keep on doing it.* That's a key. Keep on doing it and the fear will slowly subside.

When I had enough money, one of the first things I splurged on was a small boat. It was a 22-foot Center Console powerboat and I kept it docked in a scenic harbor on the south coast of Rhode Island. I loved the name that was already on the boat, so I kept it -- *Dreamcatcher.*

Ironically, I bought it at a discount from someone who was going through a nasty divorce and had placed an ad in the paper. But his bad fortune had become my good fortune, and now it was mine, and it instantly became my fort on the water. And I intended to use it just like that fort I would hide in during my childhood back in Canaan.

Buying the *Dreamcatcher* was a turning point in my life. I was drawn to it, and I viewed it as an opportunity and a tool to help me try to act normal. I tried to project a glamorous image as a true yachtsman without a care in the world.

I figured if I could pretend to be normal, my abnormal feelings would drift away. I remember paying for the boat, putting it in the slip, and going over all the details with the seller. It was a Friday, and I was a bit more relaxed than usual, as I knew I was looking ahead to three days of freedom playing with my new "fort on the water", before I had to suck it up again and start my anxiety-ridden work week. I pretended that I knew a lot more than I did about the vessel, and boating in general, and the seller eventually said goodbye and left me standing alone in the cockpit.

Like many states, Rhode Island doesn't require you have a boater's license. So I looked out across the dock past the marina, untied all three lines and started the engine. Slowly, I made my way out of the dock and through the guide buoys. I had been on boats before, so I figured I knew what I *should* be doing. The water was calm so I kept my idle speed low. I steered with one hand and while waving at other boaters and pleasure seekers with my other.

I was relaxed. The Thing was nowhere in sight. My anxiety level dropped from three, to two, to one. I felt like I had been doing this my entire life. It was natural. I believed I was meant to be here.

As I passed through the breakwater at the rocky inlet of the marina, I found myself in Block Island Sound. I looked to my left, then to my right, and could see nothing but dark blue ocean clear to the horizon. The water was no longer as calm as it was in the cove, and two to three foot waves now slapped against the side of the boat, causing it to rock a bit. I then realized I was completely alone.

The beast was stirring. My anxiety levels surged upward from a level one to a level five.

I started to worry that I had been too cocky back at the dock and that I shouldn't have pretended I knew what I was doing. I probably shouldn't have pretended that I was normal in the first place.

Despite the anxiety that was building in my mind, I pushed forward and headed out into open water.

I could have turned back, but subconsciously, I was testing myself. I was trying to learn how much I could take. I motored along cautiously for about a mile, then looked back and saw an ominous bank of fog slowly rolling in. I hadn't told anyone I would be out here today. I had placed myself in a vulnerable position and the Thing wanted to drown me.

"What if the engine quits?" the beast whispered in my ear. *"What if you have to swim to shore? Where is the shore? Why wait for the inevitable to happen? Just slip over the side and end it all."*

I felt my throat start to close, and my heart began to race.

I scrambled around the boat on all fours looking for a bag to hyperventilate into. There wasn't anything. I was angry that I didn't think to bring one along. Suddenly I pulled myself up and grabbed the wheel. I would not let the Thing bring me to a level 10. I refused to let it kill me.

"The worst is over," I shouted. "I made it. Now it's time to find my way home."

I turned the boat around and focused solely on the task at hand. I navigated back toward the marina and could think of nothing except getting beyond the rocky entrance of the break wall and back into safety. As I entered the cove, I tried to convince myself that the water was too rough out there anyway -- turning back had been the right thing to do. I quickly found my slip and re-tied the boat to the dock. Then I went about washing it down as if I had been out on a three-day cruise, smiling and waving to anyone who might walk by, trying to make it look like I was a savvy veteran boater with decades of experience. I was faking it -- just like I did in my car, on the road, and basically everywhere. But as I stood there portraying the character, I thought about what lie I would tell Robbie when I got home.

"It was a blast! I cruised all the way to Block Island, circled around it, and came all the way back. It was great. I loved every minute of it!"

Did I expect the ocean water to wash away over twenty years of the anxiety and panic I had experienced on land? Did I expect to see hospital signs posted on buoys out there and EMT's floating by ready to assist me? I recognized my ego, the fight, and my stupidity all rolled into one moment. The depression was numbing.

And that's another branch of the anxiety tree -- depression. It can't really be called a true emotion because it wraps itself around so many other feelings. It depressed me to know that I had achieved so much in my life yet I still didn't have the one thing I really wanted -- peace of mind.

There's a song by the band *Boston* called *Peace of Mind,* that I sing to myself often.

I understand about indecision

But I don't care if I get behind

People livin' in competition

All I want is to have my peace of mind.

Music has always helped me fight off bouts of depression.

Peace of Mind is a great song about a guy trying to live out his life and yearning for inner peace and balance.

It's something that I strive for but understand that I will never attain because of the Thing, this parasite that penetrates my mind. The closest I would get to inner peace was the ability to successfully tame the beast. It's something that I wrestle with every minute of every day.

But I was obsessed with fighting it. I went back out in my boat a few days later. It was early in the morning and my anxiety level was at seven even before I even set foot on the dock. I had been obsessing about the trip all night. The weather was warm, the sun was shining and the wind was dead calm. It was better conditions than anyone could hope to ask for. The night before, I bragged to everyone about how great my day on the water was going to be and about how I couldn't wait to get out there. Yet deep down, I was praying that it would rain and give me yet another lame excuse to have to stay home.

So that morning I played the *Rocky* theme once more, shouted at myself in the mirror, and used every self-motivational technique any testosterone-filled maniac would use to get going. My heart was pounding at two hundred beats per minute, yet I kept pushing myself and took the boat deeper and deeper out into the calm, majestic waters of Block Island Sound. I had decided that on this voyage, I would test myself and take myself to the very edge, and accepted that this time, I might not be able to return.

I thought about my employees who relied on me at the office, and most of all my family who loved me. I had to get over this. But more importantly than that, I had to understand this Thing.

I took a deep breath and looked down at the ignition key. I was about to cut the engine, inducing my panic in an attempt to lure the beast out of its cave.

The engine was humming in a soothing rhythm. I thought of Rocky talking to his son. How could I do this? What's the worst that could happen? What if I can't restart the boat? What if the motor just turns over and over and over again?

"Take the hits," I told myself. "Absorb and endure the pain and fear."

It was time to find out if I could break the sound barrier of fear and explore that point of no return.

It was time to be stuck in that tunnel, or on top of that bridge, or in an elevator or to have a full-fledged panic attack in front of those 20 customers in that conference room.

I turned the key and the engine went silent. I could hear nothing. In the distance, I could see one fishing boat probably twenty miles away and it was unlikely he could see me at all. I remember admiring the fisherman's resolve, and feeling jealous that he could go out anywhere he wanted -- no bad thoughts, no fears, no worries, no "what ifs" -- just go.

I breathed in the smell of the sea and the oily exhaust from the boat. All my senses were heightened.

I had a radio onboard, but I knew it would take the Coast Guard at least an hour to find me and by then I would have either hyperventilated to death or would have pounded my head into the hull of the boat until I was a bloody, dead mess. That's what the Thing wanted me to do.

I gripped the wheel until my knuckles were white, as the beast attempted to pull me away and over the side of my boat.

"Peace of mind," I muttered to myself. "You control the beast. This monster doesn't control you."

I could feel the Thing wrapping itself around my body and once again, my throat began to close. At that moment, I looked off to the golden horizon as a seagull soared over head. I breathed deeply as the rush of salt air filled my lungs.

I felt safe.

At that moment, I didn't know if I was alive or dead. I had given myself completely to the beast, and yet I felt exhilarated and free.

"No matter what happens from now on, at least you'll have this one true moment of inner peace," I said aloud. "You've pushed yourself to a near level 10 and you're okay."

In fact, I had found clarity.

I paused and turned the key to start the engine once more. It took eight to ten seconds for the boat sputtered back to life. I wept with happiness.

I thought about trying it again, but instantly created a list of excuses why I shouldn't. But it didn't matter. It was done. I had done it. It was time to move on.

For the next two and a half hours, I was normal. I brought the boat back to dock with my head held high and my chest pumped out a little farther than usual. I hopped off and started up random conversations with a couple of guys nearby. We talked and laughed about boating for over an hour. It felt wonderful.

In the movie *The Shawshank Redemption*, a prisoner who has spent his entire life behind bars finally receives his freedom. The narrator remarks with one of the most famous quotes in film history, *"He had to get busy livin' or get busy dyin'."* And sadly, the character chose to take his own life. A few scenes later Morgan Freeman's character is faced with the same decision, yet he approaches the problem differently. He elects to hop a bus and head for the ocean where he intends to live out the rest of his life in peace.

I too had to get busy livin' because dying just wasn't an option.

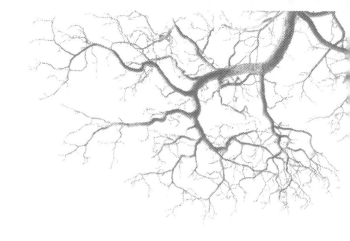

13

THE CHILDREN

"Teach your children well, Their father's hell did slowly go by, And feed them on your dreams... Don't you ever ask them why, if they told you, you will cry, So just look at them and sigh And know they love you."
— **Crosby**, *Stills & Nash*

My greatest fear has always been that I may have passed the Thing onto my children. I cannot imagine how they would be able to cope and lead productive lives of their own battling the beast on a daily basis like me. If that were the case, I'd have gladly given up my own life so that theirs could be free of severe panic and anxiety. I have an image in my head of the beast hovering over their cradles like a scene out of a Harry Potter movie. But like the child wizard, my son Michael and my daughter Jenn have been able to repel the monster thus far in their own lives.

My kids experience fear and anxiety like most other people. It hits them during moments of doubt, but it doesn't consume them like it does me.

That's partly because I was always on guard for them, both at home and during their athletic careers. If I smelled the beast around them, I made sure I was there to get them through it.

I played baseball in high school and was considered a solid player because of my work ethic. But during one game, a routine grounder sailed right through my legs and my coach screamed at me in front of my teammates, fellow classmates and parents. He humiliated me to the point where I second guessed myself in every practice and during every game for the rest of my high school career.

When I decided to coach my kids in baseball and soccer, I made sure that my instructions would be constructive. The last thing I wanted was a child to doubt his or her skills because of something I'd said.

Instead, I brought my toolbox to the field and shared with these youngsters the self-motivating techniques that I practice every day.

I exuded enthusiasm and confidence, which spread through each of my players. I had to keep the Thing in the parking lot. There's no way I could ever let it on the field. My players would have immediately read the panic on my face and in my body language, so instead I filled myself with positive energy and simply said, "play ball!".

Back when my son Michael played Little League Baseball, he would be so excited to play that he would have his uniform on and be ready to go hours before the game. It reminded me a little of me.

He was a terrific youth ballplayer, too, always playing against kids a couple of years older than him.

Two years might not sound like much of an age difference, but at that stage of physical development, it is, especially when that bigger kid is throwing a baseball at 65 miles per hour. Anyone who has ever coached or watched baseball at this level would swear that some of those 12 year olds looked like they had to be at least 18.

In Michael's first game, one of those big kids on the mound unleashed a fastball that hit him in the back. I cringed and felt his pain. Bravely, he trotted down to first base, tears streaming down his face. We checked him over and other than a bit of a red mark, thankfully, he wasn't hurt at all. It turned out to be just a glancing blow.

But as someone who suffers from anxiety and panic attacks, I had a unique insight into where my son's tears might be coming from. I worried that he would have a problem next time he batted, that he'd second guess himself like I had done decades before.

A few innings later, he was waiting on deck to bat again but he wasn't wearing a helmet and didn't have a bat in his hands.

I could read the concern on his face. I walked over to him from where I was coaching near first base.

"So Mike, are you going to hit?" I asked.

He didn't answer. He looked up at me and his tears returned. He was afraid of getting hurt again -- and understandably so. But I also sensed that his tears were being triggered by shame and the embarrassment of running away from the situation and letting me and his teammates down. In a small way, this is what anxiety and panic is all about. It's about taking a single, small fear and letting it grow into something bigger that becomes difficult or impossible to control. I knew he was not going to step back into that batter's box on his own.

"Look, if you don't want to bat anymore, that's OK," I told him. "Everyone will understand. But I also know that when you get home later, you'll be more upset. You'll be angry at yourself. And it will hurt even worse. Trust me."

I could see that he was torn. Give into the fear and go home, or step up to the plate and face it. I needed to give him a tool to guide him through this.

"I have an idea. What if you step up to the plate to hit, but just don't swing," I said. "Stand in the batter's box with the bat on your shoulder and let the pitcher throw it by you. Just go through the motions. No pressure. And do you know what? If you try it, I think you'll feel better about yourself later."

My son put on his helmet and stepped into the box. He trusted me, but I'm not sure how much he believed me, and I could see his hands were trembling. The big pitcher wound up and threw a fastball right by him for a strike as he lunged backwards. He took a deep breath, squeezed the bat a little tighter, and stepped back in for the second pitch. This time he didn't budge when it flew by.

Another fastball. Strike two. I swear I could see the anxiety melting off him.

When the pitcher's third pitch reached the plate, Michael swung and ripped a double to left field. His fear was gone. He was ecstatic. Compare that feeling to the feeling he would have had sitting at home in a self-destructive cloud of fear, anger, guilt, and embarrassment.

Years later while playing baseball in college, he always looked for me in the stands after he got a base hit and touched his heart.

My daughter Jenn was an exceptional youth soccer player, but very shy. The league's coaches were always on the lookout for the better, smarter players to help serve as game referees, and when she was asked, she was flattered and quite excited to try it.

But when we arrived at the field for her first game as an official, the reality set in that she would be overseeing girls two or three years older than she was, including many of her friends. Here she was, all dressed in her yellow uniform and ready to go to work, even with her own brand-new whistle dangling around her neck, yet she was starting to cry as we walked together toward the field.

"I'm so afraid," she confided.

So being the kind of father who was too afraid to ride an elevator or drive over a bridge, I had to find some tool or technique to help guide her through this.

"Listen," I began, "you know more about soccer than anyone else on the field today. That's why they asked you. You know you can do this."

"What if I make a bad call?" she asked. "What if my friends hate me?"

"What if you just go out on the field and run around," I suggested. "Don't think of yourself as being in charge; just make believe you are one of the players. Let the other referee make all the calls. I'll bet that after you run around a little bit, you'll feel more comfortable. In fact, don't feel like you need to blow your whistle today at all."

She was still nervous, but it helped by knowing she had my support. I believed she felt most at home on the soccer field, her safe place. And just as I had hoped, the game started and after a few minutes, Jenn took control. She did a great job.

Jenn played in college too and when she scored, I always touched my heart. That smile, no matter at 10 or 20, will never leave me.

"All my dad ever cared about was that we put in our best effort," Jenn remembers. "I would look over on the sidelines when I was playing soccer and he would hold up his hand in a way that told me I was playing at 70 or 80 percent. It was our own little language. I'd push myself until I gave 110% and my dad would place his hand over his chest. That was his way of saying that I had played with heart."

Everyone wants their children to grow to be strong, confident and successful. But when teens don't have the tools to fix their own problems, they will often turn to alcohol and drugs. It's so much harder to learn problem-solving later in life.

For me, agoraphobia has been an indescribable curse. But sometimes, my experiences with it provide a rare blessing when it allows me to teach my kids how to deal with problems without fighting them.

"My dad has taught us to live in the moment," Michael now says. "We all used to go skiing together in New Hampshire and I remember one day around sunset, we got off the ski lift at the top of the mountain. Before my sister and I could start down one of the paths, my dad pulled us together and told us to look out over the trees and onto the horizon. He held us very tight and reminded us that when things in life get sad, hard or stressful, just remember this moment and this sunset. He was right. I put that sunset in my own toolbox and use it to this day to remind myself that life is indeed beautiful."

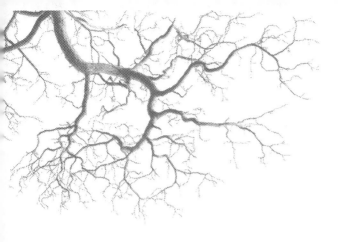

TAMING THE BEAST

"Do the thing you fear most and the death of fear is certain"
– Mark Twain

I do not believe that life's challenges are supposed to paralyze you. Instead, I believe they exist to help you learn, grow and discover who you are.

I rarely feel "anxious" anymore, but when those situations do present themselves, I prefer to use the term "uncomfortable" in its place. I hate to use the word anxious. I have accepted that anxiety and panic will never leave me completely. The Thing will always be a part of me which is why I keep my toolbox near at all times.

I have always told my kids that "life doesn't come with an instruction manual." We are living in a noisy world where everyone has an opinion to share or advice to give.

It's important to figure out in life who you should listen to and who you can trust.

For me, in business as in life, I have always valued the opinions from those who have been there and done it. I don't want to learn simply about going through the motions; I want to know about the emotional components also.

I believe that living for decades with anxiety and panic attacks qualifies me as an expert, which allows me to mentor others if nothing else.

Today when I speak to groups about agoraphobia, I can see them slide forward to the edge of their seat hanging on my every word. It's when I know I've reached them.

Therapy dogs are now placed in airports to help ease the anxiety of people who are afraid to fly. This got me thinking that I needed to explain the difference between a common fear or phobia and agoraphobia. I find that I am still uncomfortable flying and still uncomfortable when I have to speak in front of a group. But notice I used the word "uncomfortable" and not the word "afraid." When you have a fear of spiders or fear of lightning, these are fears or phobias you can both pinpoint and work on. It's when you are afraid to leave your own house and afraid of everything outside it that you reach a point that is debilitating. It is not one particular phobia. The Thing is made up of them all. It is an irrational fear of all places outside your safe place. It can't be pinpointed in the same way.

It's difficult to explain exactly what severe anxiety and panic feels like during a brief conversation with someone. I ask them to imagine the fear they would feel walking alone through a dark alley in a dangerous neighborhood -- completely lost -- with the sounds of angry dogs barking and random screams echoing in the distance. That's the level of anxiety someone with agoraphobia feels *all the time*. I have those feelings along with the terrible dread that the Thing is waiting behind a dumpster to attack in that dark alley.

It's entirely created in your mind. The beast is essentially your bad thought process at work. You are imagining all sorts of bad things that could happen to your body, you think there's something wrong with you, but your mind won't let you leave that dark, terrifying alley or in my case, the cave where the Thing lives. Accepting that these attacks cannot harm you, that they can only exhaust you, is part of the healing thought process.

Functioning while the beast is unleashed in my head has been an extraordinary experience. If you think you might be a full-fledged agoraphobic, understand that fear and panic is part of normal life. It's when these feelings escalate out of control that they become a condition that needs to be addressed, a monster that must be tamed.

Fear is a powerful emotion. Fear holds many people back. Fear can destroy your life. Everyone experiences fear on some level, but many don't know what *suffering* from fear really is all about.

I'm neither a psychiatrist nor a psychologist, but I am experienced, and you're holding my Ph.D. in your hands. I ask that you believe and trust me when I say there is a way through it, and that the other side is real. And on that other side, you can be normal again.

First, you must learn to drop your armor, the chainmail suit you wear and hide behind when an enemy attacks. The first truth you must realize and accept is that the whole healing and thought process surrounding anxiety and panic attacks will not kill you. Therefore, raising your armor to fight "the thing" is not the answer, and the sense of security your armor provides is a false one. You are only fighting yourself. Put down your shield and your sword and allow the fear to come to you. Rope-a-dope the Thing!

Feel the fear! I tested myself over and over again believing that it could become worse and lead to my eventual death. But no matter how close I came to level 10, I would never quite reach it. I could not die from it. Once you accept that these attacks are survivable, you are well on your way to recovery.

Say the words " Nobody's Coming". I wish I could remember where I first read the words "nobody's coming" because these two simple words are not only very true but have been life-changing. When I was alone on my boat, in the shower, or in an elevator, why would I always wish someone else would be there with me? Why did I want them sitting in the car with me, or standing near me in the elevator? The reason was simple. If something happened, which of course it never did, there would be someone there ready and available to call for help. I would always imagine the very worst -- passing out, choking to death, a heart attack, breathing difficulty, going crazy and even killing myself. You will learn and eventually come to appreciate that you have both the will and the power to let that fear come to you, let it pass through you, and let it leave you. You do not need anyone else. Nobody's coming -- and that's a wonderful thing -- because the healing thought process doesn't start with them, it starts with you.

Visualize the good, not the bad. I'm not the first person to advocate positive visualization, and I've come to appreciate that the reason it's so popular is because it really does work. Every time I was alone I would think about and visualize all the bad things that were about to happen to me. Why would someone *want* to think about bad things happening to them? Now, I simply close my eyes and picture myself placing a small bandage over the bad thought. There is another simple trick that worked well for me, too. I would wrap a rubber band around my wrist, and each time I realized I was having a bad thought, I would snap the rubber band hard enough to inflict a little pain, but not so hard as to break the skin. You'll be amazed at the number of bad thoughts you experience in a day. What constitutes a bad thought? Usually, they come in the form of a question intended to enhance your insecurity: "What if?" "How long will this take?"

"Will I be alone?" "How many people will be there?" "How can I get out of this?" The Thing feeds on fear and self-doubt.

Another technique is to keep a written record of all your bad thoughts for a day, breaking them down into hours and minutes. This will help you see how these thoughts have fed the roots of your anxiety tree and helped it grow. The total number of these thoughts will astound you. And it's almost incomprehensible to think about and total the number of bad thoughts you've had in your lifetime. Changing your thought process in this way is extremely hard to do, and it won't happen quickly.

The human mind is extremely powerful. Once you realize the substantial power your mind has over you, your actions and your beliefs, you can then move ahead and -- "act as if."

First you must visualize doing the right thing, then you must know it's the right thing to do, but that's still not enough. You must still actually do it.

When you stop and think about it, being scared to death is easy. The hard part is acting when you are scared. How much can you accomplish "acting as if"? Put humbly, when I think about all the bad moments I endured on all those sales trips over 30 years, yet I was still able to build a multi-million dollar business, I find it almost surreal. All the while, I did it acting as if I was normal. I still experience fear like everyone else of course, but it's a normal brand of fear like fear of the unknown, fear for your kids' safety, or fear of your own health. These fears are in no way debilitating. When you can walk, and act, you become the person you've always wanted to be. It's at that moment that you'll realize you've made it -- physically, mentally, professionally, financially and most important -- emotionally. It's OK to not fear everything every minute of every day. Act as if you want to do it. Act like who you want to become. Your mind has truly amazing power. Just act as if...

The longer you have suffered from anxiety and panic attacks, the longer it will take you to go through this healing thought process. It's as simple as that. Think about how long you've been affected by your own anxiety and fear and think about how intense those moments were. Give yourself permission to take your time with the healing thought process. Remember, getting mad at yourself is a negative thought -- snap that elastic band! Act as if. Be happy. Be patient and the negative thoughts will subside.

As I worked my way through the healing thought process, there were many times that I assumed I was healed, that it was all over. But the Thing never leaves you. It must be accepted. It is part of the process. You might feel great for as long as six months or more, only to have that damned anxiety tree rear its ugly tentacles out of nowhere. It's demoralizing, but it's not failure.

At 58 years-old, even with full knowledge of this process and how it works, I still have bad thought days where the beast gets the better of me. I no longer have to worry about selling to new customers, having dinner in restaurants, going to movies, or travelling. But I still become uncomfortable flying or speaking in front of large groups. One way that I get through it is by telling people about it. I learned that despite the number of people out there who don't fear flying, there are many that do. Feeling that you are not alone can help.

I've been there and understand the physical and emotional wars of agoraphobia, but that doesn't mean I would ever discredit the advice of any psychiatrist or psychologist; in fact, I encourage and welcome it because it is needed. The lessons I've learned and what I've been through is a gateway and path, I believe, that was chosen specifically for me. I was raised Catholic, and I do believe in God. I consider myself a spiritual person and believe that we all need help from someone, or from somewhere, at certain times in our lives.

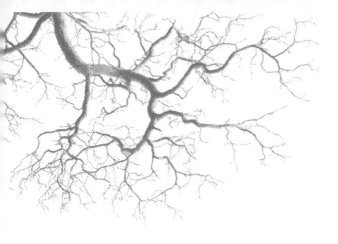

THE PHYSICAL
TOOLBOX

"Exercise to stimulate, not to annihilate. The world wasn't formed in

a day, and neither were we. Set small goals and build upon them."

— **Lee Haney**, *9 time Mr. Olympia*

My toolbox is packed with both mental and physical exercises.

A key physical element of anxiety is adrenaline -- a hormone (also known as epinephrine) that is produced by your adrenal glands and is released into your bloodstream when you find yourself in a frightening situation. Adrenaline assists the body with the increase of blood flow to muscles, the output of the heart, and increases your blood sugar, among many other things. It is the centerpiece of the "flight or fight response" inherent in all of us. We rely on adrenaline to quickly escape a burning building in the middle of the night, fight off an attacker, or run from a wild animal. In agoraphobics, the subconscious mind can open up that adrenal gland at any time whether it's needed to react to real danger or not.

When I was flying, I wanted to do as many physically distracting things as I could to reduce that impending release of adrenaline. I thought about asking flight attendants if they'd let me do push-ups in the aisles, and thought about squeezing myself into those little toilets to do sit-ups, too. But this obviously wasn't practical. I would be forced to spend my time sitting still, challenging myself with small pieces of paper, keeping my mind busy, and avoiding the pitfalls of the Thing and its dreaded "what ifs."

Through weightlifting, I created what I called Intense Focus Training (IFT), which helped engage and direct the adrenaline and cortisol in my system. This training is similar to putting blinders on a horse -- it allows you to focus your training on one particular activity, one particular set, one particular rep, and one particular moment in time while blocking out all the distracting stimuli around you. My physical training philosophy hasn't changed since my early twenties, except that now my thought process allows me to use this tool to alleviate anxiety while becoming physically stronger and mentally tougher together. Utilizing this IFT training, I can focus all my energy on one lift, or one moment, at a time.

To be honest, I can't take complete credit for this approach as many bodybuilders and weightlifters through the years have successfully implemented elements of this training technique, including Arnold Schwarzenegger, Franco Colombo, Mike Katz, and Mike Mentzer among many others. However, the weightlifter who most closely identifies with my own workout philosophy is six-time Mr. Olympia bodybuilding champion Dorian Yates.

Yates was able to summarize my own thinking with one simple analogy -- hammering a nail into a piece of wood. Essentially, he sees training as driving that nail. Once it is all the way into the wood, if you keep hitting it, you only damage the wood. The nail can move no further, therefore once you've finished, move on. Stop hitting that nail. When I first read this analogy I thought, "Wow! That's what I've been doing mentally, in my own head!" I realized that I had been using this technique for over 15 years to focus on any single issue -- a new customer, a meeting, any specific fear, or anything I wanted to succeed at doing, except I wasn't stopping, I was still hitting that nail over and over again. I would visualize what I wanted to accomplish except I would over train and ultimately fail.

Reaching goals such as adding more weight or taking another rep on a particular exercise gave me the confidence I needed to use my adrenaline when and where I was supposed to. This is where I needed my fight response to be. To this day, I still get that very same feeling when I enter my gym. These days I lift alone in my own gym, but I still continue to try and compete with my own personal bests and break physical barriers.

Breaking these barriers has enabled my mind to understand the difference between when adrenalin, anxiety, and control is necessary -- and when it is not.

This example of IFT training, in addition to my healing thought process, has helped me focus on one goal at a time, reach it, and move on to the next.

When you weight train, your goal is to overload your muscles so they replenish themselves and grow. Yates' philosophy has helped me because by the end of my workout, I realized this overtraining would cause anxiety, not alleviate it. I thought by doing more I would release more adrenaline. It was quite the contrary. I realized the nail was in the wood. I needed to stop before I damaged the wood any further.

Over the course of my anxiety and panic-filled life, I never truly understood how and why I was driven to weight training other than to get bigger, stronger, more confident, and walk around with an ego. As I got older I got smarter, and came to realize I was intentionally exhausting my adrenal glands, but in a good way. Essentially I was giving those overactive glands something to do without teasing or confronting the Thing.

I have always said that if I was able to lift weights just before meeting a new customer, the adrenaline would be dissipated and I would feel normal. Instead, I would go into meetings and sales calls exploding with anxiety. And there was certainly no way I could stop and bench press for a while in the hallway, in the elevator, or on the tarmac of an airport.

I learned to use my time in the gym to focus on the release of adrenaline to fight against the weight I was lifting. I found that by focusing my workouts in this way, my intensity level in the gym became incredible and it helped me move more weight than ever before. As I started to develop my healing thought process, I used IFT to push myself in the gym and get rid of the leftover adrenaline. By competing against myself and pushing harder to break even the smallest of personal records, I was both exhausted and exhilarated by the time I was done with each workout.

It's important to remember that the way you train and the thought process you use to train is not just about getting in shape – that's a byproduct of the IFT training method. My technique focuses on how to release that adrenaline by pushing yourself harder and faster in a short period of time, a training technique that as it has turned out, I have been doing for over 30 years without even knowing it.

Whether I am on vacation, whether I stay out late, or whether I travel for business, I will never miss a workout. I will get up at 4 o'clock in the morning if I need to, or I will train at 12 o'clock at night; it is now part of my personal make-up. My wife used to laugh at me when I would drive home from New York and then immediately go down in the basement and run on the treadmill. I did this to release the built-up adrenaline and it would help me sleep and keep the beast at bay. When you realize the effect your mind can have over body, and how this IFT training method works, you will not want to miss a workout no matter where you might be. Training heavy, training hard, and training with intensity happens to be my way to release adrenaline... but it doesn't have to be yours. Just be physical.

I still train using intense focus methods, and for those people who don't lift weights, it is just as easy to get the adrenaline and other hormones rushing through your system by using nothing more than push-ups, sit-ups and your own body weight. I am not a personal trainer, but I have many years of experience training and my philosophies have been proven by others who are. Muscle tension, isometrics, weightlifting, bodybuilding... whatever you call it, it's all you against you. And essentially it's the adrenaline that's pushing you to walk, jog, run, or exercise and push you one more rep, or one more mile.

Some people claim that simple exercise can help ease anxiety and panic, and they are not totally wrong. But it's helpful to understand the reasons behind it. I believe using exercise and incorporating these IFT principles is far more productive and effective than blindly working out. Remember that anxiety starts mentally then evolves into physical reaction. If you utilize smart physical activities along with these IFT principles and place your complete focus on any fear, small or large while training, it will work to ease your anxiety. I'm living proof. You will be teaching your adrenal glands how to work the correct way and give you control, helping you go over that bridge, through that tunnel or run that extra mile.

Get on a treadmill, do some push-ups, or go to the gym. What you do isn't that important. But use that time to not only become more physically fit and healthy, but use it to also overcome and control your panic. I am stronger and healthier today at 58 years old than I've been at any time in my life. And I'm panic free. This power has changed my life.

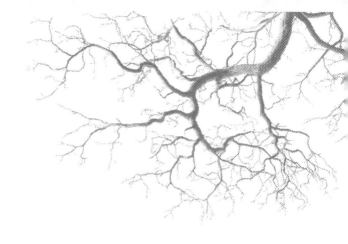

16

IT NEVER
REALLY GOES
AWAY

The whole secret to existence is to have no fear.
Never fear what will become of you, depend on no one.
Only the moment you reject all help are you freed.
~ **Buddha**

No matter how successful you become at managing agoraphobia, there is one sad truth that you will not be able to escape. It never goes away. The Thing is always there.

I am reminded of a song by Nickleback, "Feelin' Way Too Damn Good." I play the drums as a hobby and I've listened to thousands of songs. Most of the time, the lyrics escape me as I focus on the drummer working out the beat in the background. But sometimes the lyrics stick and offer me real meaning.

I feel like I'm constantly dreaming.

'Cause something's gotta go wrong.

'Cause I'm feeling way too damn good.

We have a summer home on Cape Cod and are able to spend a good deal of time there as a family. Of all the places I've been fortunate enough to visit, I think the Cape has to be my favorite. I exhale each time that I drive over the Sagamore Bridge to our little slice of paradise. But even paradise can be littered with psychological pot-holes.

A few years ago, I drove my motorcycle to the Cape to get our house ready for a long holiday weekend. As I rode, I felt at ease, smiling with anticipation. Up ahead, I could see traffic thickening and the steel buttresses of the Sagamore Bridge appearing overhead right on schedule. Suddenly I started to feel unexpectedly anxious. Was it the summer heat? The traffic? I couldn't be sure, but I could feel my anxiety level starting to climb. I started to focus on my fear of bridges, and yet I hadn't been remotely bothered by a trip over this bridge in over ten years. Then I realized that when I got to the house, I would be all alone. My anxiety level continued to climb.

I became angry at myself. I stopped at a red light and pounded the handles of the bike with my fists. I had started to fight it just like I did when I was in my twenties. Old habits are hard to break.

"What the hell, Brian, I thought we were done with this?" I shouted into my motorcycle helmet.

I gripped the motorcycle handles tighter and as I approached the bridge I could feel my body physically shaking. My fight or flight response was in full operational mode. I had released the Thing.

In the old days, I would have stopped. I might have turned around and headed home, telling the family that I was sick, or that the motorcycle was broken. But on this day, I was equipped with the tools I needed to repair this breakdown. I began to focus on a favorite quote, "Truth is always the companion of calm."

I've learned to have that toolbox ready at all times, wherever I go, as I never know when the "The Thing" will decide to spring on me. I have learned to harness the power of my subconscious mind, which is far more powerful than you think, to engage my healing thought process.

In less than three minutes, my anxiety level dropped from five... to four... to three... to two. I began to realize that I was the victim, again, of my own bad thoughts. There had been some problems the day before at work, and I had stayed up far too late the night before at a party, so I was working on two to three hours of sleep at best and had been pounding the caffeine that morning. Just like a virus that attacks when you're tired and your immune system is down, bad thoughts do the same. No matter how cured you think you are, those bad thoughts are out there lurking, waiting for you to let down your guard.

So I turned that bad thought process into a good thought process. I said to myself, "this is only anxiety. I won't die from this. I've been over this bridge a hundred times..." I prepared to "act as if." I thought about the fun we would have that weekend. I smiled. My positive thoughts soon overwhelmed the negative ones.

As the anxiety started to escape my body, I experienced a tingling feeling all over. The more I smiled, the better I felt. My fingers loosened their grip on the handlebars, and I said aloud, "it was only anxiety." I was relieved that everything in my toolbox was there to help me.

The biggest step is recognizing that it's only anxiety, nothing more. Years ago, I would have followed that realization with, "Yeah, but..." And now today, the thought doesn't cross my mind because I know the tools are there, and like that old screwdriver you might not need for years, my confidence rises just knowing I can rattle around in there and pull it out whenever I need it.

The whole experience only lasted three or four minutes; in the old days, it might have lasted hours. As I moved ahead to finish the remaining twenty-four miles of my journey toward my house, traffic eased and the temperature dipped to a perfect 78 degrees. In just two miles, I was happy and normal again.

Anxiety and panic will never go away for me completely. I will experience it the rest of my life. And that's OK.

Acceptance is what keeps all the other tools within the healing thought process together, safe inside, and ready to use.

For decades, I tried to hide my affliction from Robbie and the kids and did so successfully. I feared showing any vulnerability because I thought it would make me look weak. Today, I know that the strong seek help, and that we are all battling our own version of the Thing. Writing this book has opened a new chapter in the relationship with my wife, who has stuck by my side for decades. I worked so hard to shield her from this beast inside my head that I wasn't being truly honest to myself or to her.

"When I started reading the first pages of the manuscript, I sat and cried," Robbie explains. "I never knew the extent of what Brian was going through."

Robbie began to analyze my past behavior, showering right when I got home from a sales call or the need to work out immediately when I returned from a long drive or trip.

"I feel like I should have seen the signs," she says. "But I didn't."

It's not Robbie's fault. She was married to a man who'd spent his entire life fooling himself and others into thinking that I was "normal". I wore this disguise each and every day because I felt that I needed to be strong for my family. I should have understood that Robbie and the kids would have accepted me for who I am. Their support has been truly incredible.

"This isn't Brian's fight any longer," Robbie explains. "We are all in this together. I hope that families will recognize the symptoms that Brian has shared so honestly in these pages and compare them with the anxious behavior of their children or their loved ones. Brian never got the help he needed as a child or young man. His story can serve as a cautionary tale for others."

My wife is right. For me, writing this book was an introspective journey into both my past and my mind. No longer could I dismiss the Thing and force myself to believe it didn't exist. I wanted to visualize it for myself and for others to understand the beast that resides in the psychosis of an agoraphobic like me.

I spend a lot of time alone these days. Some people might think that makes me a loner, but it's far from the truth. I used to fear loneliness. I needed to have others around to maintain my sanity.

Where I am in my life now, I have learned to enjoy being alone with my thoughts. It's not like it used to be. And these are normal thoughts, by the way, they're not thoughts of despair, anguish, depression or those dreaded "what ifs."

I close my eyes and imagine that I'm on my boat at night as I circle a buoy at Conanicut Point near the Beavertail Light here in the waters of Narragansett Bay. It is so dark I can barely see my hand in front of my face, and the ocean air is heavy, humid and warm. I reach down and switch off the engine of my boat -- but this is not a test. The testing is over! This is a moment of joy.

I peer through the darkness to the south across the Atlantic, the boat is gently bobbing up and down and suddenly I see the dim lights of another boat -- perhaps a tanker -- many miles away. I am sitting at the stern, caught up in a very spiritual moment, thinking about how lucky I am, how far I've come, and how exciting and rich my life truly is.

For years, people have seen my success from afar and said, *"man... I wish I was you"* and I fought them. *"Oh, yeah? Do you have any idea what I went through?"*

But I consider myself blessed and I am grateful for everything in my life. I have travelled over highways and byways, through the air thousands of miles to build my business, while living every moment in fear and terror. I have spent countless nights crying alone in my room, or hunched over the steering wheel in my car, covered by a shroud of anxiety and self-doubt. All because I was panic-stricken and I could not show my fear.

But the beast does not reside in Robbie's smile. The Thing cannot be found in the voices of my children when we laugh together. The dark, looming anxiety tree is blocked out by the sun and pruned by joy. There is hope for all of us living with agoraphobia. Life can indeed be good if we all recognize our vulnerabilities, our fears and work to overcome them. It's okay to be *Scared to Death*. But remember my story and do it anyway.

Printed in the United States
By Bookmasters